Murder in
Notting Hill

Murder in Notting Hill

Mark Olden

Winchester, UK
Washington, USA

First published by Zero Books, 2011
Zero Books is an imprint of John Hunt Publishing Ltd., Laurel House, Station Approach,
Alresford, Hants, SO24 9JH, UK
office1@o-books.net
www.o-books.com

For distributor details and how to order please visit the 'Ordering' section on our website.

Text copyright: Mark Olden 2010

ISBN: 978 1 84694 536 6

A CIP catalogue record for this book is available from the British Library.

Design: Stuart Davies

Cover photo: Detectives search a drain for the knife that killed Kelso Cochrane.
Copyright: Mirrorpix.

Printed in the UK by CPI Antony Rowe
Printed in the USA by Offset Paperback Mfrs, Inc

We operate a distinctive and ethical publishing philosophy in all
areas of our business, from our global network of authors to
production and worldwide distribution.

CONTENTS

For my late father Andrew Ray, whose face was known throughout the Grove.

Her heart would fill with dread when she heard the key in the door. Had he been in a punch-up? Was he about to pick on her? If he was in a good mood, she'd do her best to keep it going. If he was pissed, she'd give him another drink, hoping he'd pass out. She was on edge when he was around, and felt the tension lift when he went. "Thank God that bastard's gone," she'd think.

She was only young, but even then she found him hard to fathom: how he didn't seem to have any fear, how everything was always a grin, how he had lots of friends, but didn't trust any of them.

When his mates came round, he and her mum would get her out of the way, probably because she was the kid who answered back. But sitting by the banisters on the stairs, she'd eavesdrop on their conversations, and always knew more than she let on. Sometimes, if she played the fool or started the singing off, they'd let her stay.

She couldn't remember exactly when she first heard it. Coloured people often had weird names, she thought, and she often got the first syllable wrong. But it was a name that stalked him. A name his friends mentioned every now and then with knowing looks and sly comments, usually when the drink had been flowing.

Elso. Oslo. Kelso.

He would fix them with a glare, and speaking through his teeth in that way of his, say: "Shut your mouth. I don't know what you're talking about."

PROLOGUE

Sunday May 17, 1959. It was late when the phone rang at the *Sunday Express*. Frank Draper, a junior reporter on night shift, reached for it. When he was interviewed by the police five weeks later, this was how he described the conversation that followed:

"Are you interested in a murder?"

The caller's voice was rough and hesitant, and he sounded a bit like Johnny Carter, a criminal known for tipping off newspapers with stories. Draper thought the man might be drunk. Placing his hand over the mouthpiece he asked a colleague's advice, before returning to the call.

"Three white youths have stabbed a darkie named Cochrane on Golborne Road, Notting Hill."

The informant refused to give his name, but around an hour later *Murder in Notting Hill* was the banner headline on the front page of the paper's 4am edition.

* * *

Saturday May 16, 1959. Packed coaches left Victoria Station at the rate of 100 an hour and the roads out of London were clogged with traffic. It was the warmest Whitsun Bank Holiday in years, and people were leaving the city in droves. With more sunshine forecast, the newspapers predicted the "biggest bumper-to-bumper weekend Britain had ever known".

Kelso Cochrane had the more mundane matter of a hospital appointment to attend. In the morning he had the plaster re-cast on his broken left thumb, which he'd injured in a fall at work on Wednesday. The fracture was relatively unusual - of the base of the first segment - and the doctor had struggled to shift it back in position.

When Kelso was done at the hospital, he met his girlfriend. At

21, Olivia Ellington was 11 years his junior, and five weeks before, the trainee nurse with the fresh, round face had moved into his rented room at 11 Bevington Road, at the northern end of Portobello Road.

In the afternoon, the couple went shopping at the market around the corner from their home. They passed the antique stalls, the raucous barrow boys selling fruit and veg, and the street traders hawking old clothes and trinkets, and got back at 4.30pm.

Afterwards, Kelso's younger brother Malcolm arrived, and the men talked and shared a bottle of ginger wine. Then Kelso set aside £3 for the landlord and they all left: Malcolm went to his home in Stoke Newington, Kelso and Olivia headed for Hyde Park to hear the soap-box orators at Speaker's Corner.

By the time they returned, they were ready for bed. But Kelso was restless. The pain in his thumb was agonising. Olivia suggested codeine. Although he had an appointment to see the doctor again on Monday, Kelso couldn't wait: he wanted it treated immediately.

He emptied the loose change from his pockets on to the dressing table by the bed, and set out for Paddington General Hospital, a converted Victorian workhouse just over a mile away on Harrow Road. As usual, he was smartly dressed: in blue trousers, an open-necked grey and black striped shirt over a vest, a brown jacket and brown suede shoes.

In the following days the police re-traced Kelso's journey that night, and discovered that the area around his route was buzzing with activity during the critical time.

Turning immediately right into Golborne Road, he walked past The Mitre pub. Since the afternoon 50 guests had celebrated a young white couple's wedding reception there. At the top of the road, on Hazelwood Crescent, some black people were holding a birthday party, which also continued until late. Two hundred yards from the junction with Golborne Road, in the front room on the ground floor in a terraced house on Southam Street, locals drank at an all-night get-together.

Nearby, the normal Saturday night disturbances filled the police logs: violence at a party at 165 Westbourne Park Road; a car broken into on Tavistock Road; a girl assaulted near Hospital Lodge on Green Road; a 23-year-old man arrested for hitting two policemen while trying to resist arrest on Talbot Grove; and further north, by Kilburn, reports of youths fighting between Quex and Smyrna Roads.

Sometime after 10.30pm, Kelso passed the uniformed porter manning the hospital's front gate, strolled the hundred yards across the frontage and entered Paddington General. He waited a while before being called in to see John Givans, a courteous young doctor on twenty-four hour shift who'd already treated him that morning. Dr Givans later described the patient as pleasant, friendly and sober. He remembered him smiling despite the discomfort of his injury. Givans prescribed strong pain killers and told Kelso not to take them until he got home.

It was before midnight when Kelso left the hospital. A few minutes later he approached the junction of Southam Street and Golborne Road, the plaster over his left hand visible in the street lights. Fifty yards away, a black cab was dropping off four passengers. Two men drunkenly debated who would pay the fare while their female companions clambered out of the car. Kelso's home was five minutes away.

Through the window of a first-floor flat, a young woman and her mother saw what happened.

A gang of white youths closed in on the black man, surrounding him. There was pushing and jostling as he tried to defend himself with one hand. It was over quickly. Kelso fell outside The Bagwash Laundry, by a Vehicles Prohibited sign, and a few yards from a blue public police phone box linking directly to Harrow Road police station. A single stab with a very sharply pointed, sharply edged knife had penetrated the main

3

chamber of his heart.

* * *

"A chill breeze sweeps the street corners of Notting Hill and adjoining North Kensington, ruffling the duck-tailed haircuts of the knots of white youths who stand there, eyeing their coloured neighbours as they pass," wrote Arthur Cook in Monday's *Daily Mail*. *"The coloureds quicken their pace as they go by. On just such a street corner one of their number was knifed to death the night before...Kelso Cochrane became the first fatality in the colour 'war' that flares intermittently in the seamy side of the Royal Borough of Kensington...From a house a short way along the street walked two quietly-dressed young white men. 'I don't want my name in this. I'm 25 and want to get out of this place soon.' ...What did they think about the trouble the night before? 'If a coloured boy's been killed, that's one less, and it suits us. The whole 4,000 of them should be cleared out.' Across Golborne Road the Earl of Warwick was filling with Sunday lunchtime drinkers. Nora, the pianist, was playing the old favourites and an elderly woman was taking round the hat...The jokes and banter were forced, in between talk of the night before and the looming question: 'What's going to happen now?'"*

* * *

Wednesday May 20, 1959. At 12.45hrs a telegram marked "IMMEDIATE" and "CONFIDENTIAL" was sent from the Colonial Office in Whitehall to Lord Hailes, Britain's Governor General of the West Indies, in Port of Spain, Trinidad: *"...Police in Notting Hill have been doubled...Very close watch generally is being kept...Prompt and severe measures would be taken if there were signs of trouble developing..."*

As the authorities moved to prevent any unrest, campaigners mobilised around the death of the 32-year-old carpenter from

The victim: Kelso Cochrane.
Copyright: Getty Images.

Antigua, whose life was laid out in a few, sparse details in the newspapers. Quiet, hard-working, he earned £15 a week, was engaged to marry Olivia Ellington and liked his jazz, especially Ella Fitzgerald, they said.

Within twenty four hours of his death, the Committee of African Organisations held an emergency meeting in London and sent an open letter to Prime Minister Harold Macmillan, in which they connected the killing to the racial violence infecting America's Deep South. The Notting Hill crime, it read: "rivals what we have seen at Little Rock or the recent lynching of Mr M C Parker of Poplarville, Mississippi." Three weeks before, Mack Charles Parker, a black man accused of raping a white woman, had been abducted from his Mississippi jail cell by white men in hoods who beat and shot him dead.

The next day, the Labour MP Barbara Castle also linked the stabbing on Southam Street to faraway troubles: in this instance the brutal deaths in British custody two months before of Mau Mau rebels fighting colonial rule in Kenya. "If the British people are going to allow those responsible for the beating of 11 detainees to death in the Hola concentration camp in Kenya to go untraced and unpunished we shall have given the green light to every 'nigger-baiting' Teddy Boy in Notting Hill," she said.

On Sunday May 24, Dr Carl La Corbiniere, Deputy Prime Minister of the West Indies Federation, flew into England on a two-month mission investigating the causes of racial tension: "I think you will find it almost impossible to convince any West Indian that this was not a racial murder," he told the press at the airport. Special Branch, the police unit concerned with national security, had already dispatched someone to keep a watch on events. In his report the officer noted: "The murder of the West Indian attracted considerable public attention in the West Indies."

By Wednesday May 27, the campaigners were building momentum. They'd formed a new organisation in response to the murder - the Inter-Racial Friendship Co-ordinating Council - and a nine-strong delegation from the group spent an hour at the Home Office appealing to a senior civil servant for a new law banning incitement to racial hatred. Among the activists were Claudia Jones, the Trinidadian-born communist who'd been jailed in America during the McCarthy witch-hunts, and Amy Ashwood Garvey, the ex-wife of the black nationalist leader Marcus Garvey. "The eyes of the world are on Notting Hill and the good name of Britain as a democratic nation, in which all can live together in mutual respect, equality and dignity is in danger of being smirched by the actions of a small minority of thugs holding a fascist ideology which millions of men and women died in the last war to wipe out," stated the group's memo to Home Secretary Rab Butler (dutifully transcribed by Special Branch).

More than 500 people crammed St Pancras Town Hall the next night for the "We Mourn Cochrane" public meeting, which started at 7pm. "The thing I am most afraid of," proclaimed Father Trevor Huddleston, speaking beneath a twice life-size painting of the victim, "is the appalling silence of the good people who by their positions of power and authority could rally public opinion if they wanted." For 13 years Huddleston had ministered in South Africa's shanty towns, and had been threatened with imprisonment and deportation by the apartheid regime. For him, the gravity of the situation could hardly be exaggerated. "Within this country we have the seeds of a racial discrimination that could be an absolute disaster to the future of Great Britain...Colour discrimination is the supreme issue of our generation," he said. Dr La Corbiniere also spoke, pronouncing the murder "a tragic incident in the history of the world".

"The meeting passed off quietly," the Special Branch observer recorded, and that same night Moscow Radio broadcast a report on Notting Hill to its African listeners entitled *Racism Rages in London*. "That savage murder was premeditated. There is no quiet in London these days," said the presenter.

Then, starting at 6am the following Monday, half a dozen anti-racist activists staged a vigil by the heart of Britain's political power. Two policemen stood stiffly by as members of the Coloured People's Progressive Association marched in single file and a few feet apart, slowly up and down Whitehall. They passed the corner of Downing Street and the Cenotaph, where poppies lay commemorating the war dead. They'd wanted to carry a black coffin with a red dagger sticking out, but the police said this could be seen as incitement, so instead they held placards.

"Only one race – the human race."

"Decent people of Notting Hill speak out against the colour bar."

"Racial Discrimination should be illegal."

"Murder in Notting Hill."

A white man in a loose-fitting suit attached his - declaring *"No Little Rock here"* - around his neck with a piece of string, while a slim black man held a drawing of Kelso. For 12 hours they kept on, undeterred by a burst of lunchtime rain, but attracting scant interest from passers-by, as the city's rhythm continued undisturbed around them. "We are making this protest to find out who our supporters are. We want to know who will stop talking and do something," one of the organisers said.

Finally, the Home Secretary was moved to speak. On Thursday June 4, with Kelso's brother Malcolm watching intently from the public gallery, Rab Butler rose in the House of Commons. "I would appeal to anyone who can help the police in their investigation of this deplorable murder of a coloured man in Notting Hill to do so," he said. "Racial discrimination has no place in our law, and responsible opinion everywhere will condemn any attempt to foment it." MPs murmured their approval. Appealing in the Mother of Parliaments for witnesses in a murder was unprecedented said the papers the next day, who also reported that Butler was "considering the recruitment of coloured police as part of his campaign to end racial tension".

Saturday June 6, 1959. Half an hour before the funeral, hundreds of people, both black and white, congregated around St Michael and All Angels, a small, foreboding brick church on Ladbroke Grove, with semi-circular arches framing its doors and windows, and a roof shaped like the top of a barn.

A white man wearing dark glasses and a black armband wandered unobtrusively through the crowd selling newspapers, a cigarette dangling from his mouth. A matronly white lady in a headscarf clasped her right arm round the shoulder of a small white boy, her left around a black boy of roughly the same age. There were young white men in immaculate suits and Asian women in saris; black men in tuxedos and black women clad in bright summer dresses with patches sewn on their sleeves as symbols of mourning.

The wreaths piled up. *The Government and People of Liberia* had sent one, so had *The Martyrs and Victims of Oppression - Nyasaland*. *"Ever loving Kelso,"* read the black-bordered card on another, *"Your death was by the hand of a blind man. His terrible deed has opened many eyes and drawn innumerable warm hearts in love towards you and yours."*

Watching under a clear sky were dozens of police: on foot, in vans and patrol cars. The casket, draped in a royal mauve-and-gold cloth, was taken from the hearse. Two pallbearers stumbled momentarily, but their colleagues quickly steadied the coffin before carrying it into the church, which was so full that the police had stopped people from entering. The lesson was read by the Bishop of Kensington. *"Oh death, where is thy sting? Oh grave, where is thy victory?"* he asked, and the mourners sang the hymn 'For all the Saints who from their labours rest'. At the front, tears streaming down her face, sat Olivia Ellington.

When the service was over, the crowd bunched behind the cortège, waiting for it to begin its journey up to Kensal Green Cemetery. Around 1,000 people made their way north up Ladbroke Grove's steady incline. By the time the procession reached the gates of the cemetery - passing two hundred yards from the murder spot - it stretched half a mile back.

Once inside, people perched on tombstones to get a clearer view, keeping their balance by grasping the overhead trees. The coffin was lowered into the earth and a few rushed forward, breaking past the line of stewards. A lone voice broke into *Abide with Me*, before others joined in, and it swelled to a choir. For an hour afterwards, 500 people remained by the graveside singing hymns.

"Black hands clasped white as the mourners quietly dispersed. The absence of bitterness and the determination of the organised coloured people had made it a deeply moving occasion," said *The Daily Worker* newspaper.

"Many people were in tears," said *The Times*.

There was one minor incident. A tall black man in a skull-cap and flowing white robes was led away by three policemen and questioned for 15 minutes at the lodge at the front of cemetery. They'd seen him distributing pink leaflets about a meeting called for 1.30pm the next day.

"IT COULD BE YOU!!! Kelso's murder is Britain's shame. All Africans and Afro-Asians must make this Sunday a day of remembrance for a dear brother who was murdered because of the colour of his skin," they said. The man's name was Sherriff Sesay, and in their report Special Branch described him as *"a prominent coloured communist"*.

The following day, 400 people marched in honour of Kelso from Hyde Park Corner to Trafalgar Square, where Sesay announced plans to erect a statue in his honour in Antigua.

Three weeks had elapsed since the murder. Kelso Cochrane's name was known across the world, his image frozen in the endlessly reproduced portrait of him staring impassively at the camera through half-rimmed spectacles. His funeral had been more like a revered statesman's than an unknown carpenter's, and his death had become a rallying point for those of all races opposed to discrimination. The *News of the World* had even offered a £2,500 reward for the capture of his killer, announcing on its front page that "no clue is too small to be considered in solving the Kelso Cochrane murder, and *News of the World* readers who believe they can throw any light on the killing should contact their local police station immediately." Yet the police appeared no closer to finding the culprit.

* * *

March 2003. As he got older, Stanley Cochrane's sleep was becoming increasingly erratic. There were nights when he awoke after dreaming of Kelso; restless hours when thoughts of his brother's violent death wouldn't leave, and when the question of who killed him, and why the police never caught them, kept churning over. The next day he'd feel agitated.

"I was short and snappy at anyone I came into contact with, because these things were worrying me," he said. "All human beings deserve justice. They can't just be snuffed out like some animal. Don't you deserve justice if you suddenly disappear without provocation? He was cut down in the prime of his life. Cut down like a dog."

These thoughts had long been there, but in his seventies they nagged at him with greater intensity. Before, Stanley had a family to raise and a career to focus on, first in the Civil Service in Antigua, then as a denturist in Canada - while as a Jehovah's Witness, his spare time was spent knocking on doors distributing *The Watchtower*. Now he dwelt on all the years Kelso - three years his senior - never had.

He remembered their childhood in Johnson's Point, a village with dirt roads and no electricity on the southwest tip of Antigua. Their house stood out among the 20 or so mostly-thatched homes. Their dad had built it with his own hands, and it was so solid it would have taken a cyclone to tear it apart. Just across from where they lived, on the other side of a little mangrove swamp, was a sandy white beach and the crystal blue sea where the country's early inhabitants, the Arawaks and the Caribs, fished centuries before Europeans transported African slaves to the island, and where Stanley, Kelso and their brothers, Eustace, Fitz and Malcolm, would splash about and hold swimming races.

There were eleven siblings and half-siblings in all, and Kelso was the strongest. "Kelso was tall, not bulky, athletic. He was a good fighter. He could defend himself. You couldn't overcome him easily in battles," Stanley recalled. Their upbringing was strict. "My father always emphasised that we're not to steal and we're not to disrespect anyone. And in those days if you were to go off course and disrespect someone in the street, that person would probably give you a little whipping. And if you go home and you tell your dad you'd get another whipping."

Odd, vivid memories remained, such as Kelso and him in their dad's workshop, taking turns rotating a bicycle wheel attached to a pulley, which drove the lathe their dad honed his latest work with. Furniture, wheels, ships and boats, Stanley Cochrane senior made them all.

As the boys grew, it was Kelso who took up the family trade, working with his dad as a shipwright, while Stanley pursued his education. When he was nineteen, Kelso moved to Dominica and earned his living as a carpenter, before returning to Johnson's Point three years later. He was ambitious but opportunities at home were scarce, so in September 1949 he upped again, this time to America. After labouring on a farm in Florida, he briefly joined the US army, and then married a woman from South Carolina called Kansas Green, with whom he had a daughter, Josephine. They lived in New York, where Kelso studied and where he was financially assisted by two uncles, one of them a lawyer - a profession Kelso had dreams of pursuing.

But within two years his marriage descended into serious

acrimony, and his visa expired. On February 19 1954, he arrived back in Antigua on a Pan American Airways flight, deported "on the grounds that he had remained in the US beyond the period for which he was admitted".

Although he'd been granted permission to re-apply for entry to America, England beckoned. Antigua was part of the British Empire, and Kelso Cochrane was therefore a Citizen of the United Kingdom and Colonies. He'd arrived back from New York with little money, so he turned to Stanley.

"He was building a house for his mother. The house was partially finished, and he came to me because I was earning. So I gave him the passage money and he said I could keep the house and finish it, and use that towards part of the money I gave him," Stanley remembered.

Kelso's last few years had been turbulent, but this was a new beginning. Boarding the French liner Colombie at Point-à-Pitre in Guadaloupe, he listed his occupation as carpenter, his last place of permanent residence as New York, and his proposed address in the United Kingdom as Liverpool.

The 500-passenger ship had begun its journey at La Guaria, Venezuela, picking up mostly male travellers at various West Indies ports, before heading across the Atlantic and arriving several weeks later, on September 4, 1954, in Plymouth, England.

Almost five years later, a man pedalled six miles on a bicycle from Antigua's capital St John's to Johnson's Point carrying a telegram with the shattering news.

"I heard that one of his hands was in a sling of some kind," said Stanley. "He had some damage done to his hand. Even though there were six [attackers], if Kelso wasn't incapacitated he would have been able to defend himself. He was very good at defending himself in the village." Stanley couldn't go to England for the funeral. "We weren't paid much in the Civil Service, and at the time I also had to contribute to the rest of the family because my dad had left to work in Trinidad."

Now, as he got older, he realised he knew nothing about chunks of his brother's life. "There was a gap from when he left the country to the time he died that I have no knowledge about. These gaps, you have to fill them somehow. You have to come to a period of time when you're going to be satisfied emotionally."

He'd lobbied the Antiguan Prime Minister to take up Kelso's case when he visited England in 1968, and nothing came of it. But at 3am on an especially disturbed night in March 2003, Stanley Cochrane rose from his bed in Alberta, sat down and drafted a letter to the Metropolitan Police Commissioner, Sir John Stevens. No-one had been brought to justice for the murder, he wrote, and Kelso's surviving relatives were still distressed by it. He wanted the case re-opened.

"I thought this was the time when I had the energy and the money to spend to come to England if I had to," he said. "Scotland Yard is a very efficient organisation. We are of the opinion there is nothing that they cannot discover. I wanted to know if they'd made a reasonable effort to find the perpetrator."

CHAPTER ONE

ONE FOOT IN THE GROVE

"We gain our knowledge of life in catastrophic form. History is written after catastrophes...The death has taken place. What had been brewing beforehand? What had happened? Why has a situation arisen? All this can now be deduced." Bertolt Brecht.

From its affluent south to its deprived north, there have always been two Notting Hills, if we call the rough triangle of London W10 and W11 by that name, rather than its official North Kensington. Of all the district's tribes, the roots of the white working-class of Notting Dale probably run the deepest.

With its border west of Ladbroke Grove's busy main artery and north of the grand Victorian townhouses of Holland Park, the Dale was first populated by a succession of brick-makers, pig farmers and seasonal gypsies. From the beginning, overcrowding and poverty went hand in hand.

"In a neighbourhood studded thickly with elegant villas and mansions, [Notting Dale] is a plague spot, scarcely equalled for its insalubrity by any other in London," an article in Charles Dickens' *Household Words* journal pronounced in 1850. Writing when the Irish Potato Famine was near its end, the author noted: "In these hovels discontent, dirt, filth and misery are unsurpassed by anything even known in Ireland."

According to an official report from the same period, it was said that: "The inhabitants all look unhealthy...with shrunk and shrivelled skin the women particularly complaining of sickness and want of appetite." This was the time a cholera outbreak saw deaths rise in a community already besieged by smallpox, diphtheria, typhoid and scarlet fever. Pigs outnumbered humans and infant mortality was more than 50 per cent.

With lives so bleak, no wonder many sought oblivion in alcohol. According to the book *Notting Hill in bygone days*, the physical intensity of their work led the brick-makers of the Dale "to drink at least seven pints of beer a day", and by 1904, the cramped cluster of streets at the heart of the neighbourhood had one public house to every 25 dwellings. "Bad housing and the inherited effects of alcoholism, improvidence and vice tended to sap the vitality of the sons and daughters of the Dale," the writer curtly noted.

By the 1950s, Notting Dale was a place of tight-knit clans with deep tribal loyalties, where everyone seemed to be bound by blood or marriage, and a whole family could be found living in a single room in a crumbling tenement with no bathroom and an outside toilet. "Save for a few bourgeois enclaves," wrote the novelist Colin MacInnes at around this time, it was "a rotting slum of a sharp, horrible vivacity...The citizens, among whom a criminal element is traditional, live on the streets, in a way rare even in prosperous working-class areas."

The pig-masters and brick-makers were long gone by then. In their place came casual labourers, factory workers and rag-and-bone men who collected junk in horse-drawn carts. Bookies' runners patrolled the street corners, dustmen and milkmen took bets as a sideline, and costermongers sold fruit and veg in the nearby Portobello market. The very name 'Portobello' conjured such ghastly connotations for Notting Hill's posh residents that they mounted a campaign to have it changed on account of its "notoriety" and "unpleasant characteristics".

Old tyres and rubbish lined the pavements, and the area was dotted with scrap yards and used car lots - useful fronts for petty crime. Illegal gambling dens known as *spiels*, and drinking clubs known as *afters*, appeared faster than the law could close them. The fiddles were endlessly inventive: robbing your own gas meter, and cutting off bits of lino to shove in the money slot until there was nothing left covering the floor; and, with an ingenuity rivalling that of the ancient Greeks who discovered static electricity by rubbing amber with silk, the story goes that some people sourced their electricity from the street-lamps outside. But while the Dale had more than its share of cadgers and thieves, it's also said that you could leave your door fastened with just a piece of string and nothing would get stolen.

Those were the days of sugar sandwiches for tea, of gas-lit streets and old ladies - as well as old men - in flat caps. It was summer afternoons lazing on the front steps, and evenings getting suited and booted and heading to the pub for sing-alongs and late-night lock-ins. Once a week you'd scrub yourself down in a cubicle at Silchester Baths. If you called for more hot water, old man Hoskins would strain to turn the bolt, and out it would gush. You could get a mug of tea and bread pudding there, have a natter, and if you paid a shilling they'd give your clothes an extra boil. On Saturdays it was the pictures at The Electric on Portobello Road, commonly known as 'The Bughole'. The man in the box office had a missing index finger, the seats were wooden, and the shows were regularly disrupted by an attendant spraying disinfectant.

Naturally, people had their squabbles. Good fighters were respected though, and if two lads were scrapping, it was thought better to leave them to get on with it and shake hands after-wards, than intervene and let the bad blood fester. But if an outsider went for one of the local boys, people would rush to defend them. In the Dale you looked out for one another, and strangers - even from nearby Shepherd's Bush - were viewed warily.

So when foreigners from thousands of miles away and of a different race arrived in Notting Hill in increasing numbers throughout the 1950s, such deeply-entrenched suspicions were amplified.

* * *

In truth, black people had lived in the area for centuries.

The first recorded black resident in what was later called the Royal Borough of Kensington and Chelsea, was 'Charles', a Guyanese boy baptised in the Parish of St Luke in 1597, and brought to England by the Elizabethan adventurer Sir Walter Raleigh. For the next 350 years, there was a steady black presence in the district. Among the bodies found after one German bombing raid during the Blitz, for instance, was that of Frederick Pease, an actor who lived in plush St George's Square, and who was described as having "negroid features".

But it was after the old troop-carrying freighter known as the Empire Windrush pulled into Tilbury Docks in Essex on June 22 1948 carrying five hundred Jamaicans, that the story of black Britain changed forever. In the next ten years, 125,000 West Indians arrived.

They came on the promise of jobs that couldn't be filled, having been reared on the idea of the Mother Country and an Empire on which the sun never set, on tales of heroic deeds by Admirals and Generals, and the belief that in Britain all were treated equally. Such notions proved as vaporous as the London fog. When you went for a job, you were either over-qualified or under-qualified - or somehow both. When you tried to rent a room, the room had either gone, or the rent had gone up. But there were some areas, essentially ghettoes, where a roof could be found: The Bay in Cardiff, The Meadows in Nottingham, Manchester's North Side, and in London - Brixton, parts of the East End, and Notting Hill, commonly known as the Grove.

The corner of the Grove it was easiest to find somewhere to live was Colville. Just east of Notting Dale, on the other side of Ladbroke Grove, its four and five-storey Victorian houses had been built in the 1860s by property developers eager to cash in on London's growing population. They had long since fallen into ruin, with cracked front pillars, paint-starved exteriors and corroding balconies. Inside, thin walls divided the houses into multiple bedsits and flatlets, allowing ever more tenants to cram themselves in.

To cover the rent, four or five of you might live in one dank, dismal little room, and if you worked days and your room-mate nights, you'd take turns in the bed. In winter you'd all hunch round the paraffin heater, and if you left your milk in the sink overnight it would still be cold in the morning. You'd cook your scrags, the meaty neck of the lamb which wasn't popular with white people and was therefore cheap, on a single ring gas hob on the landing. By the time you'd paid your bus fare to work, shelled out for your lunch when you got there, shoved a few shillings in the meter when you got home (fumbling around in the dark if the lights had suddenly cut out in the process) your pockets were empty.

Back then you'd wave if you saw another black man on the road, but as more people from the Caribbean settled in Notting Hill, and Colville became known as Brown Town, that would have meant waving every few yards. In no time, there was something happening around every corner.

There was Roy Stewart's basement gym at 32a Powis Square, which doubled as a late-night unlicensed drinking club. Roy arrived from Jamaica in 1948 with dreams of becoming a doctor, but after appearing as a snake-charmer in a Fry's Turkish Delight advert on TV, supplemented his club earnings with work as a film extra and a stuntman. Unlike the white extras he succeeded, the powerfully-built Roy didn't wear make-up to play Zulu warriors.

There was The Apollo on All Saints Road, where the landlord only served blacks in the public and not the saloon bar - until he saw how much money he could make and changed his policy. Soon black people were coming from all over London to drink there.

The Rio at 127 Westbourne Park Road was open seven days a week and most nights, and was decorated with fishing nets the Trinidadian proprietor Frank Crichlow acquired on a trip to Southend. Hustlers in Zoot suits mingled with white women and the odd middle-class bohemian slumming it.

Sarah Churchill, Sir Winston's actress daughter, was a regular at Totobags, a cafe and community centre also known as the Fortress, where a mostly Jamaican crowd played dominos and cards until the early hours, and where she indulged her taste for black men while her chauffeur waited patiently in the Rolls Royce outside with his cap pulled over his face.

And then there were the *shebeens*: the illicit clubs which sprang up in people's homes, where you could drink, smoke dope, play poker, and let the latest rhythm 'n' blues pumped through purpose-built speakers wash away the week's worries.

Soon, Colville's reputation was set: for many it was merely somewhere to stay while they grinded out a living and gained a foothold in a new, cold land; for others it was a place of wild possibility, of vitality and decay, where going out at four in the afternoon and coming home at five the next morning was the norm.

Friday August 15, 1958. Over the past year the situation had deteriorated. Violence, hooliganism and minor thefts had risen. Some people were too scared to talk. Others were threatening to take matters into their own hands. "This," declared the *Kensington News*, "is the gathering storm in Ladbroke Grove." The newspaper listed the underlying causes. Landlords were taking advantage of the 1957 Rent Act - which had loosened statutory controls - and were pushing up rents and throwing out tenants. 'Mushroom' clubs were appearing one night and disappearing the next, blasting music through portable juke boxes until the early hours. "Then there is the much more serious problem of growing hostility towards coloured people."

"Unless something drastic is done soon, I don't know what the consequences will be," one resident warned. "The situation here could easily lead to violence of the worst kind," said another.

"These young men were trapped within a history; being both weak and violent, they could not escape from it."
Dan Jacobson, *After Notting Hill.*

Sunday August 24, 1958. In the hours when Saturday night became Sunday morning, the streets of west London proved more hazardous than ever before for black men. The first attack came after 2am.

MacDonald Waldron, a kitchen porter at the catering firm J. Lyons and Co., left a party with a white girl and was nearing Ladbroke Grove station when a white man came up and shoved him to the ground. He struggled to his feet, but was knocked down again. He heard shouting and felt a crack on his head. Later, at the casualty department of St Charles' Hospital just off Ladbroke Grove, six stitches were put in his skull. He was concussed and bleeding from the nose.

Some forty-five minutes later, Matthew Lucien and his friend John Pirmal approached 254 Lancaster Road, where they shared furnished accommodation. Lucien worked on the railways. Pirmal had arrived from Trinidad two months before and was seeking work. They'd missed the last train after wandering around the West End, but were almost home - and very close to where Waldron had just been attacked. A black, pre-war Singer drew up and out piled a gang of white youths who immediately laid into the black men. Lucien escaped. Finding his path blocked, Pirmal turned to flee in the other direction and tripped. Shortly afterwards, the youths drove off, leaving him on the pavement. They were so tightly squeezed into the Singer that some were clinging on to its sides. Pirmal had been stabbed.

The night doctor at St Charles' treated a half-inch long puncture wound on the right side of his chest and inserted five stitches in his head. Lucien had evaded serious injury, with a small bump on his scalp and a bruised shoulder.

A little over an hour later and a couple of miles west, Joseph Welsh, a North Thames Gas Board labourer, made his way home along Shepherd's Bush Green. The black Singer appeared on the other side of the Uxbridge Road. The next thing Welsh knew a white man bounded across the grass and punched him in the face. Welsh hit back but the assailant was joined by a white gang. When he was later seen by the night doctor at St Charles', Welsh was found to be concussed, and had three cuts on his head requiring nine stitches and bruising on his left knee and right elbow.

Still the youths in the Singer weren't done. One mile north and daylight was breaking, as James Ettiene headed down Wood Lane towards North Pole Road twenty minutes after finishing his night-shift for London Transport. The Singer drove up but Ettiene barely registered it. Then he felt a blow on the back of his head, and started to run. The pack gave chase: they were screaming and armed with sticks, iron railings and a knife. "No," yelled Ettiene, "I've just finished work." Reaching a milk crate, he lobbed bottles at his pursuers, and then leapt on to a passing trolley bus. As it moved away, two youths jumped on. "Throw the nigger off" one ordered the conductress. He was holding a lump of wood. She ignored him, and when the bus stopped by a public police phone box the youths sloped off and the driver called the police.

Ettiene was treated at Hammersmith Hospital for an abrasion on his right temple, bruising on the left side of his breast bone and bruising on his right arm.

At 5.40am PC Eric Wilding spotted the black Singer heading west along the Uxbridge Road with around nine youths somehow crushed inside. The car turned right into Stanlake Road. The policeman stopped a passing taxi and told the driver to follow it. A few minutes later he saw it parked by the barrier at Batman Close on the edge of the White City Estate, with the youths milling about. As Wilding jumped out of the cab, one of them shouted "The Law!" and they scattered among the rows of public housing blocks.

PC Wilding drove the car to Shepherd's Bush police station, where it was found to contain a makeshift armoury comprising of a table leg, an air pistol, several iron bars with spear-shaped ends torn from street railings, a crank used to start car engines, and four pieces of green painted wood.

The next day at 1.25pm, a 17-year-old labourer from the White City Estate walked into Shepherd's Bush station and reported that he'd lost a black Singer, index no DGO 221 from Australia Road, W12. He produced the car's log book and was promptly held for questioning.

Eight other youths were soon traced. They were mostly from around White City and Shepherd's Bush. One was from Notting Dale. The youngest was 17 and the oldest 20. Only one had previous convictions, for relatively minor offences. They came, on the whole, from decent homes and had regular employment; the highest earner among them was already on ten guineas a week.

From Sunday evening through to the early hours of Monday morning they were interviewed separately under caution at Notting Hill station. The accounts the nine gave of the night before barely varied in the essential details. Nor did the casual descriptions of their violence: as if beating random black men senseless was as acceptable as kicking a ball in the park. The evening had begun aimlessly enough, as the 17-year-old from Notting Dale explained:

"Last night I went with Nipper, Johnny and Bobby in Johnny's old car to Denham. We only went for a ride, it was something to do. We got back about 11 or 11.30pm. The pubs were closed. We came out of the City down Marble Arch, Piccadilly Circus and then back along Oxford Street to Bayswater Road down to the Bush."

"We stopped at that stall at the end of the market and had something

to eat. None of us were drunk, in fact [we] hadn't had a drink all night. We then drove along Uxbridge Road and saw Tony. He was with about six or seven other fellows. I don't know them by their names, except one is Little Teddy, another is Ron, and another one is Frank. I think it is. I asked them where they were going and they said, 'We are going spade-hunting'...I knew they meant to go out and look for niggers and belt them."

A 17-year-old who lived with his parents in Shepherd's Bush and worked as a printer's apprentice at Westminster Bank - where his employers spoke 'very highly' of him - said: *"Last Saturday night I had taken a girl home and was on my way back when I met Ted, he was on his own. Then we bumped into some mates of ours and they said they were going out in a car hunting niggers."*

There was a lone dissenting voice: the owner of the black Singer, according to the Dale youth: *"Johnny said 'You can't all get in this car'. They all started to call him a snuffer and that, so Johnny got needled and told them to all get in. They did and we all drove off towards Kensal Town by the iron bridge. The electrics thing on the car was sort of ticking, so Johnny said it wanted some petrol. We had a bit of a whip-round and then we had seven or eight bob."*

"We all got out leaving Johnny, Wagger, Bobby and Nipper in the car," said a 19-year-old window cleaner from Hanwell. *"They said they would go and get petrol and meet us in Ladbroke Grove under the iron bridge."*

While their four friends filled the car up at Rootes garage on Barlby Road, the others went and joined an Irishman they'd never met before in their first attack of the night, on MacDonald Waldron.

According to the Westminster Bank worker: *"We saw that Paddy having a fight with a nigger, there was another nigger standing looking on. We went over and had the nigger who was looking on but he got away. The other one got a right paying."*

"We set about the two niggers and they had it away quick," said an 18-year-old labourer who lived with his brother in

Hammersmith. *"The white bloke, who I have never seen before was Irish and he joined up with us. The car came back and we got in it."*

Bolstered by their four friends, the group spotted their next victims: John Pirmal and Matthew Lucien.

"We saw two more niggers walking along Lancaster Road near the KPH [the Kensington Park Hotel pub on Ladbroke Grove]. One of the boys shouted over to the niggers 'black cunt' or something like that…We all got out and we gave the niggers a belting. At least one of them got a belting, the other one got away," said the Dale youth. *"I only hit him once or twice with my bit of wood,"* added the Hanwell window cleaner.

The oldest of the group was a 20-year-old who'd served as a gunner in the Royal Artillery in Cyprus and been discharged with a 'very good character'. He told the police: *"Then we all went in the car to Queensway. A nigger was walking along the road and Paddy jumped out and set about him. He ran away and some of the fellows threw wooden sticks at him."*

They drove west to Shepherd's Bush, where they spotted Joseph Welsh. *"We saw a nigger strutting along the road as if he owned the world,"* said a 17-year-old scrap metal merchant labourer. *"Somebody hit him and we all got out and hit him. He trotted off. Then we went up Wood Lane and a nigger there started chucking bottles at us and he jumped on a bus. We followed the bus down and the driver stopped by a police phone box and we went on."*

"I am a mug to get lumbered into this," moaned a 17-year-old greengrocer from White City, *"but these niggers keep on taking liberties with us…I swear on the bible that although I joined in giving the niggers a whacking I had nothing to do with any stabbing."*

"I don't like niggers because they insulted an old girlfriend of mine and because of the bad way they behave with women," said the Westminster Bank worker. His statement was read over to him by Detective Inspector A. Fernie, before he signed it. Its final words were: *"I don't like niggers."*

A few days later, the nine were up at West London

Magistrate's Court, where the day invariably began with ER
Guest, the long-serving magistrate with piercing eyes and a
sharp tongue, passing judgement on a steady stream of drunks,
prostitutes and petty thieves. When John Pirmal, the youths'
second victim, was carried in on a stretcher, Guest was flabber-
gasted. "I have never seen a man brought into court in such a
state," he said.

Detective Sergeant Maurice Walters of Notting Hill said the
police objected to bail because of "the serious nature of the
charges [and] the likelihood of the accused taking part in similar
incidents against coloured people." The defendants were taken to
Wormwood Scrubs Boys Prison and committed for trial at the
Old Bailey in three weeks. By the time their case came to court,
the gathering storm that the *Kensington News* warned of had
burst.

* * *

Friday August 29, 1958. It's generally agreed that some of the
worst rioting in Britain in the last century was triggered by a
quarrel between a Swedish wife and her Jamaican husband.

On a mild summer evening Majbritt and Raymond Morrison
stood arguing outside Latimer Road tube station. She had mouse
blonde hair, was 26-years-old and pregnant. Soon she would be
working the streets as a prostitute. Raymond was a fine looking
man with a pencil-slim moustache, and a gifted artist who'd
worked in a hospital when he first arrived in England. Now he
earned his living as a pimp. They'd met three years earlier, when
she was visiting London with a group of Swedish students.

As they squabbled, people stopped to gawp, including white
men who shouted at Raymond in defence of Majbritt. Majbritt
turned on them, taking her husband's side. The row turned into a
scuffle, and when Raymond's West Indian friends arrived, the
scuffle became a fight. No-one was hurt, but that night in pubs

and clubs around the Dale, people spoke with one voice in words dripping with venom: they were going to teach the "schwartzers" a lesson once and for all.

The following evening, a local Jamaican character known as King Dick was holding a blues party on Blechynden Street. Majbritt went for an hour or so before walking home, which was just around the corner in Bramley Road. At 11.50pm she turned into her street and saw the fire brigade and police cars with flashing beacons and a mob of 100 or so. The first-floor flat she shared with Raymond had been set alight.

As she ran towards her house a young Teddy Boy recognised her. "There's another black man's trollop," he shouted. "Get her. Kill her." Majbritt made it to the front door and dashed inside to search for her two cats, who she found cowering behind the sofa. Then she returned to face the crowd. "Is it blood you want?" she asked. "Kill me, but don't start anything."

A large youth smashed her back with an iron bar and she almost fainted. An elderly white man came to her defence. "Can't you see the woman is carrying a child," he said. Steadying herself, Majbritt was ordered back inside for her own safety by Police Sergeant Douglas Shearn, who was on guard at her front door. She ignored him, and he arrested her for obstruction. The police drove her to Notting Hill station where she was detained until 5am.

The horde, meanwhile, had turned their attention to Blechynden Street. As they drew near King Dick's packed blues party, their din drowned out the strains of Oriental Ball, the calypso tune playing at that moment. King Dick looked out from the top floor window, saw the baying crowd below and heard their chants. "Kill the niggers." "Go home you black bastards." Seconds later, bricks and bottles rained on the house. An all-out attack was averted by the arrival of the police, who escorted the revellers to safety. The disruption to King Dick and his friends' night was only temporary, and they resumed their party at an address on Lancaster Road.

The Notting Hill race riots had begun.

Over the days and nights that followed, a kind of madness gripped the district. Lone black men were chased and beaten. White men marched the streets armed with razors, butchers' knives, bicycle chains, knuckle-dusters, weighted belts and dustbin lids. The hospitals and police cells filled, as the press and outsiders streamed in. The police struggled to contain the crowds, which at times stretched back 200 yards. Yet even in the midst of all the violence, reported the man from *The Times*, white housewives were *"looking after their coloured neighbours' babies and doing their shopping for them"*, and *"white and coloured children [were] playing together"* in the streets.

Monday September 1, 1958. Darkness was falling when the West Indians struck back. Three hundred of them had barricaded themselves into two houses on Blenheim Crescent, just over the Colville side of the Grove: the women were at number six; the men across the road at number nine, in Totobags community centre. The men had prepared for this moment throughout the day: filling up petrol cans at the station on Kensington Park Road, and buying tools at Carpenter's hardware shop on Portobello Road.

Their attackers came from Bramley Road, passing through Oxford Gardens, before making their way down Ladbroke Grove and turning left into Blenheim Crescent just after 9pm. In the West Indian citadels the lights were off and the curtains drawn. Somebody shouted: "Let's burn the niggers out". It was then that the first Molotov cocktail - a bottle of flaming sand and petrol - was hurled from the fourth floor of Totobags. More petrol bombs followed, along with a hail of bricks and iron bars. Most of the white rioters fled to Ladbroke Grove, where they continued causing havoc by the station. The few stragglers who remained ran between the houses throwing missiles, before disappearing when some black men emerged from Totobags waving meat cleavers and machetes.

There had been fears that the contagion would spread to other parts of the metropolis with sizeable black populations, but although there were reports of fighting in nearby Shepherd's Bush and Paddington, the Siege of Blenheim Crescent - as the *Daily Mail* called it the next day - marked the beginning of the end. The police, who'd mounted one of their biggest operations of the decade, started to prevail.

Wednesday September 3, 1958. It rained from the early afternoon through to the middle of the next morning. For once, Notting Hill's pubs were virtually empty and the few drinkers who ventured out were heard talking about football. At 9.30pm the thunder crackled and the heavens opened again, deterring further trouble. One hundred and eight people - 72 white and 36 black - were charged with offences ranging from using insulting or threatening behaviour, to grievous bodily harm and possessing offensive weapons. Most of the white men were under twenty, and in the papers' convenient shorthand, were branded Teddy Boys. Despite numerous serious injuries, remarkably, no-one had been killed.

* * *

Notting Hill was far from Britain's first large-scale race riot. In fact, the week before, blacks and whites had clashed in St Ann's, Nottingham, with more than 1,000 people marauding through the city's streets.

And forty years before that, in Cardiff in June 1919, white men demobbed after the First World War formed lynch mobs to attack black sailors living in the city's boarding houses. Three whites and one Arab were killed. *"Revolvers [were] freely used and casualties caused by bullets, razors, sticks and stones,"* reported the *Manchester Guardian. "The causes of the tumult are attributed to the license given to loose women in well-defined areas to congregate and solicit black men, and the consequent resentment of white men."*

In the same month, Liverpool was also beset by racial violence, and up to 700 black people were locked up in Bridewell Prison: *"to protect them from the fury of the white mob, which for several days have been attacking the quarter in which the black population is concentrated,"* said *The New York Times*. By mid-September the government had repatriated 600 black people to Africa and the West Indies.

But while they weren't unprecedented, Notting Hill's disturbances nevertheless sparked fevered debate across the world.

Jamaica's Chief Minister Norman Manley said that they had profoundly affected the struggle for racial decency. "It is much more tragic than Little Rock for the West," he stated, referring to the landmark segregation case in Arkansas the year before, when the State Governor ordered the National Guard to stop nine black students attending an all-white high school, and President Eisenhower responded by sending in the 101st Airborne Division to escort them into the building.

A columnist in the *New York Herald Tribune* detected hidden, malevolent forces, suggesting that Notting Hill's riots were the product of a communist conspiracy. And in South Africa, the pro-apartheid *Die Burger* newspaper argued that Britain's racial upheavals would breed "a humble desire for true knowledge" among public and politicians.

British politicians and their civil servants were already deeply exercised by events. "A comprehensive Immigration Bill is being urgently studied by officials of the Home Office," said a confidential report by a government working party. The number of new arrivals from India and Pakistan had dropped sharply in the past few months due to tougher passport controls in those countries, it said. "The immediate problem, then, is to restrict immigration from the West Indies."

* * *

Monday September 15, 1958. Light fell into the Old Bailey court room through a circular glass roof. The defence made their pleas and the clerk told the nine youths who'd roamed the streets of west London "nigger-hunting" the week before the riots to stand.

They had, wrote the author Dan Jacobson, the *"pinched, pale faces of English city boys - faces on which the lips and eyes look vividly dark, everything else having no colour."* They were: *"small, thin, thin-wristed, thin-necked...[there were] only two of them that one could imagine being able to attack anyone bigger than a schoolboy in a playground...you could have seen them on a building lot, riding a delivery boy's bicycle, being a mate to an electrician: you wouldn't have looked twice...they weren't sunken nobodies, they were rather jaunty anybodies. And that was the most disturbing thing..."*

Seated in a heavy green leather chair and wearing a wig and scarlet gown, Mr Justice Salmon, presiding over his first Old Bailey case, began reading the prepared speech that would take him seven minutes to complete, and which would be printed in huge bold letters across the front-page of the next day's *Daily Mirror.*

"...Your object was to instill stark terror and inflict as much pain and grievous injury as you could. During that night, you savagely attacked five peaceful and law-abiding citizens without any shadow of an excuse. None of them had done you any harm. None of them had given you the slightest provocation. Indeed, you knew nothing about any of them except that their skin happened to be a colour of which you, apparently, didn't approve. It was you men who started the whole of this violence in Notting Hill. You are a minute and insignificant section of the population who have brought shame on the district in which you live, and have filled the whole nation with horror, indignation and disgust.

Everyone, irrespective of the colour of their skins, is entitled to walk through our streets in peace with their heads erect and free from fear. That is a right which these courts will always unfailingly uphold. As

*far as the law is concerned you are entitled to think what you like,
however foul your thoughts; to feel what you like, however brutal and
debased your emotions; to say what you like, providing you do not
infringe the rights of others or imperil the Queen's peace, but once you
translate your dark thoughts and brutal feelings into savage acts such
as these, the law will be swift to punish you, the guilty, and protect your
victims."*

Salmon wasn't even half-way through when one boy's mother
started crying, and when he passed sentence, gasps of disbelief
were heard from the public gallery. A blonde woman stood and
started waving her arms as if she'd witnessed some terrible
carnage, before being ushered out in tears. The nine youths had
been given four years.

There was confusion on the street outside. A small man in a
tight blue suit shouted: "Four years! My boy's life is ruined..." By
the time the news reached west London, however, the mood had
darkened. Salmon was a communist, a nigger-lover, people said.
A letter threatening to shoot him, signed by a group claiming to
be ex-Commandos, arrived at the *Daily Mirror*.

* * *

"Some of the finest faces you could wish to see..."

At a meeting at Oxford Gardens School, just off Ladbroke Grove,
the campaign to free the nine young men was growing. A tall,
thin Welshman - rarely seen out of the same jacket and trousers -
held aloft a newspaper with their grinning portraits. "Thugs.
That's what they were called," he said. This was outrageous.
"These," he shouted, "are some of the finest faces you could wish
to see in Britain." He vowed they "must not be forgotten as they
lie in prison during the best years of their lives." Around 60
people stamped their feet and cheered. Afterwards many added
their names to a petition demanding that the four-year terms be

reviewed.

The speaker was Jeffrey Hamm. He was 43-years-old, had lived in Notting Hill for the past six years and was Secretary of a far-right political party called the Union Movement. Notting Hill was now seen as the frontline in the conflict around race and immigration in Britain, and as such, was where the UM was pouring its energies. It organised weekly public surgeries and well-attended street corner meetings there. It opened its second office, opposite a synagogue and by a kosher butcher's, at 47 Kensington Park Road. And it distributed its free four-page newsletter, the *North Kensington Leader*, to every house in the district.

"There has been a big smear campaign against North Kensington in the press of the old parties," ran a typical article. *"They tried to make Notting Hill a bad word. Why? Because you dared to object to the whole character of your neighbourhood being changed by the mass immigration of Jamaicans."*

Notting Hill was also where the UM's leader, a man once tipped as a future British Prime Minister, and hailed as "the paramount political personality in Britain" in 1934 by the *Daily Mail*, would try to resurrect a soaring political career that had long fallen into disgrace.

Tuesday October 7, 1958. For a damp, miserable week night, the turn-out at the Earl of Warwick, on the junction of Golborne Road and Southam Street, was unusually large.

"An air of expectancy hung over the public bar, and the conversation revolved around the subject of the distinguished visitor who was coming at 9.30," The *Kensington News* reported. *"'Is it true he's coming here tonight?' And 'Where has he got to?' At 9.40 the door swung open and a tall, bronzed, impressive figure of a man stood on the threshold." "Someone started to sing 'For he's a jolly good fellow' and the refrain was taken up throughout the bar."*

Sir Oswald Mosley stood in the centre of pub, his hands clasped behind his back, his eyes dilating hypnotically in trademark fashion. The leader of Britain's pre-war fascist party, and former ally of Hitler and Mussolini who was jailed during the war as a threat to national security, soaked up the rapturous welcome of the men in suits surrounding him, who concluded their final "so say all of us!" by vigorously pumping their arms.

The 62-year-old - in the breathless description of a local reporter a "soldierly figure remarkably untouched by the years" and dead-ringer for Douglas Fairbanks senior - had wanted to speak at Kensington Town Hall that night, but the council had declared that any "extremist organisation" meeting would be inadvisable, so he toured the borough instead. Over a pint he berated the local authorities for their decision. "That shows how afraid the Government and the Labour Party are by what we have to say," he said. "If they are not afraid of the truth we are speaking they would let us speak."

There was one question that Sir Oswald was repeatedly asked during his visit: Was he standing in the forthcoming General Election?

"I will stand if it is the only way to get justice for the people of North Kensington," he replied.

Monday April 6, 1959. More than 600 people filled the Argyll Hall on Lancaster Road for Sir Oswald's first public meeting as a prospective parliamentary candidate for the district. Despite some heckling during his sixty-minute oration, the Special Branch mole present described the crowd as "enthusiastic". Most of their questions afterwards were on "the colour question". On this, Mosley was emphatic: "We are determined they shall go home."

One especially zealous UM member, not from Notting Hill but living on Clysdedale Road in the Colville area, thought he knew how this vision could be achieved.

"Instead of writing moderate articles in a paper which nobody reads," he boasted to colleagues, "we should get hold of an immigrant and hang him upside-down from Blackfriar's Bridge with a notice round his neck saying 'Coloureds go home'. That would give us the publicity to kick-start the campaign and get Mosley elected." The man's words were relayed back to Sir Oswald, who summoned and rebuked him.

"Okay I was bollocksed by the old man," he told his friends back in Notting Hill. "He shouted at me and said, 'Never do that again'. Then God's truth, he looked at me and winked."

* * *

There were some on the far-right who found Oswald Mosley far too moderate - and his message about as inspiring as drizzle on a dark winter's day.

Like Jeffrey Hamm, Colin Jordan was a schoolmaster with fascist convictions. His Notting Hill base at 74 Princedale Road also happened to be a few yards away from Hamm's residence, which was at number 46. But when it came to politics, Jordan saw himself as miles apart from the Union Movement and its leaders.

A Cambridge graduate with a baby face, thinning hair and perfect diction, Jordan journeyed from his Coventry home to his Princedale Road HQ at weekends. Wire protective mesh covered the front windows, above which his organisation's name was painted in white capitals against a black backdrop: White Defence League. Full annual membership of the WDL was 10 shillings, and though the building lay dormant during the week, at weekends Jordan's small band of followers met there, donning Nazi-style regalia and playing military marching songs that eventually drew complaints from neighbours.

Jordan had acquired the property in 1956 from the widow of the late Dr Arnold Leese. A veterinary surgeon, expert in camel diseases and virulent anti-semite for whom Oswald Mosley was merely a "kosher fascist" directed by Jews, Dr Leese founded the pre-war Imperial Fascist League, and in 1947 was jailed for helping two Dutch Waffen-SS soldiers escape from a PoW camp in Epsom Downs. Like Dr Leese, Jordan saw Jewish machinations everywhere - not least in somehow orchestrating West Indian immigration to Britain. In November 1958, he began publishing *Black and White News*, a pamphlet he distributed personally on the streets of Notting Hill, and whose headlines mirrored his obsessions: "Negroes lead in VD", "Kings of the Drug Trade", "King of the Prostitutes", "Black gets White Girl".

"The National Assistance Board pays the children's allowances to the blacks for the coffee-coloured monstrosities they father, regardless of whether they are legitimate or illegitimate," said a front-page article. *"Material rewards are given to enable semi-savages to mate with the women of one of the leading civilised nations of the world...It's time to defend yourself by joining your local WHITE DEFENCE LEAGUE."*

After all, Jordan told an interviewer, *"Notting Hill, remember, is still part of England."*

CHAPTER TWO

WHITE MEN LIKE YOU

Kelso Cochrane had shifted around various addresses in Notting Hill's northern fringe, before moving into the front room on the first floor at 11 Bevington Road, W10, a freshly-painted Victorian terrace where a number of West Indians lived.

It had been almost five years since he'd set foot in England. He hadn't intended to stay. In September 1956 he applied for US citizenship with the support of his estranged American wife, and the following May his request was accepted. Soon he'd be returning to New York. But his wife met another man, withdrew her backing, and everything changed. In September 1958, Kelso entered a new relationship - with Olivia Ellington, a young Jamaican trainee nurse, who he'd been introduced to by a mutual friend called Gloria Miller. People say that Olivia and Kelso were glued to each other, and there was talk of marriage. In April 1959 she moved into his bedsit at Bevington Road. To this simple sketch, Kelso's friends from the time add some colour:

"...He was very flamboyant, I like him very much for that. He's not an arrogant fellow or anything. He makes a lot of jokes, like you'll say 'Hi Kel give me a pound'. And he'd say, 'Listen man, I'm broke as the 48 Commandments.' So you'd say, 'What is that?' and he'd reply, 'Thou shalt go no lower'..."

"...He always dressed smart. You think he's going to church all the time. A very upright man like that..."

"...A loving boy, such a nice young man. Very quiet. Always minded his own business and kept himself to himself. He played the guitar and was studying to be a lawyer..."

"...We used to have good fun because at this time people were just beginning to get married and have families and both of us were very

good in giving speeches...so we used to have a competition [to give the best speech]. You know, you're young and you don't really know the words that you use. They maybe don't have no meaning anyway..."

One thing all agree on was Kelso's closeness to his older cousin, James Christian.

"*...Kelso used to almost worship James, They adore each other...*"

"*...Anything he wanted to do, he would always get a second opinion from James...*"

James lived with his wife Rose in Hornsey, north London, an area with a high concentration of Antiguans. Kelso would visit each week, and Rose would serve him traditional food: Fungi, Okra, Rice and Peas. Sometimes Kelso spoke to them about Notting Hill. "The people are very rude down there," he would say.

Wednesday May 13, 1959. Kelso saw James and borrowed some records. He said that he'd return them within the next few days via his brother Malcolm, who lived nearby. That day Kelso was in pain. A few hours before he'd fallen while on a carpentry job, landing on his left thumb.

On Thursday he went to Paddington General Hospital with a note from his GP and had the thumb x-rayed. A fracture was diagnosed, which was reduced under general anaesthetic. But the operation was unsuccessful, so on Saturday morning Kelso had his thumb re-positioned and the plaster re-cast. It was still hurting badly in the evening. He left Olivia at home and made his way to Paddington General.

Saturday May 16, 1959. At around midnight, two Jamaican friends were walking down Golborne Road after leaving a Saturday night dance. As Horatio Lewis and Ken Steele approached the junction with Southam Street, they saw five or six white youths surrounding a black man in the dim light twenty yards away. The black man was trying to escape, but the youths had him hemmed in. There was kicking and scuffling, then one of the young men leapt from near a public police phone box on to the black man's back, and he fell to the ground. "Oi I'm here!" Steele shouted, running towards the mêlée with Lewis. The attackers had vanished by the time they arrived.

Joy Okine, a blonde, green-eyed 21-year-old clerk, was at home sewing a dress and waiting for her dad to arrive, when she and her mum were disturbed by a commotion outside the window of their first-floor flat on the corner of Golborne Road. The women peered out on to the street below, and saw a gang of youths pushing and shoving a black man. The black man was standing up for himself and one of the gang was trying to rip an iron railing from the ground to use as a weapon. The youths ran off and their victim staggered to his feet. The attackers were smartly dressed and she thought they'd been drinking.

At the same time, George Isaacs, a 45-year-old taxi driver, was dropping off four passengers outside 87 Southam Street. He too noticed the scuffle, over on the corner of the road by the Bagwash Laundry. He heard no shouting, but saw a flurry of arms, and what appeared to be coming and going, with two men leaving the group and two others joining it. One man was closer to the person being jostled than the rest. As Isaacs' two male passengers discussed who would pay the fare, the taxi driver drew their attention to the fracas fifty yards away. The passengers glanced over, drunk and disinterested. Isaacs took the money, and three young men of medium height walked very quickly by him on the opposite side of Southam Street. They were heading eastwards away from the scene. One was moving faster than the others and kept looking around.

Kelso Cochrane was slumped on the pavement when the Jamaicans reached him. Steele recognised his face from the area. As they crouched over him, two white youths appeared from behind and offered to go after the attackers. Steele said no. He didn't think Kelso was seriously hurt. The youths wandered off down Southam Street, also in an easterly direction.

The men helped Kelso to his feet and asked him what had

happened.

"They asked me for money but I told them I didn't have any," he mumbled.

Isaacs then pulled his cab up Southam Street and across to the kerb by the corner of the road. He noticed for the first time that the victim was black.

"He's just been attacked by those three white fellows," Steele explained.

Isaacs said he'd just seen them going down the road, and offered Kelso a lift home.

Kelso was fading by the second though, and had sunk to his knees and was starting to moan. They decided to get him to St Charles' Hospital, half a mile away. Lifting him into the taxi, Lewis noticed a spot of blood seeping through his shirt; it was so small, he later recalled, it could have been from a mosquito bite.

At 12.30am they arrived at St Charles'. The three men waited while Dr Mohammed Seddiq examined the patient and asked him some simple questions. All he got back was a name. Kelso was in severe shock: his pulse was weak, his skin cold and clammy, and his consciousness slipping. At 12.32am a message was sent from St Charles' to Harrow Road police station, and immediately passed on to the night duty CID officer, Detective Sergeant Sidney Coomber. Coomber was at Paddington General Hospital investigating a GBH, but rushed over to St Charles' with his colleague Detective Constable Frank Buchan, arriving in a black Hillman CID car at about 12.45am.

"I entered a cubicle where I saw a coloured man I now know as Kelso Cochrane, lying on the floor being attended by a doctor, a sister and a nurse," Coomber said in a statement later. "I assisted giving this man artificial respiration." Moments later, he was dead.

Coomber stepped outside and saw Steele and Lewis. "I told them that the man had died and on hearing this they burst into tears and started behaving violently i.e. throwing their arms about and threatening what they would do if they caught the person responsible. The nurse standing by was accidentally struck by one of the coloured men." Coomber left Lewis and Steele in the CID car with DC Buchan and then searched the dead man's clothes with the help of the night sister. "Amongst his property I found a pawnbroker's contract note, bearing the name Frederick or F. Corkrane."

The post-mortem was conducted by the Home Office pathologist Dr Donald Teare. The deceased, Teare found, was a powerfully built man of 6ft 1in and around 13 stone. His body had no natural diseases and no alcohol was found in his system. There was little blood on his clothing, but in the front of his left chest was a wound, delivered with unusual velocity. A very sharp, stiletto-type knife had been driven in horizontally, entering through the fifth rib, penetrating two inches, deep into the main chamber of the heart, thereby causing severe haemorrhaging.

"To put a knife through a man who is muscular and powerful would require considerable force," concluded the coroner.

* * *

The Pride of Hendon

The task of finding Kelso Cochrane's killer fell to Detective Superintendent Ian Forbes-Leith. Formerly on Scotland Yard's murder squad, two weeks before he'd been made head of CID in X Division, the Metropolitan Police district whose field of operations ran from the northern edge of Portobello Road up to Kilburn, and whose headquarters were a three-storey red-brick building at 325 Harrow Road. This was his first major case in his new job.

The largely working-class area he'd been thrust into was at odds with his background. Born in Totton in Hampshire, public school-educated, his manners were impeccable and his dress sense refined. With his customary bowler hat and pipe, he looked more like a city gent than a hardened detective at home in the seedy end of west London - where running an army of snouts eager to curry favour or earn a few pounds was a common means of cracking cases.

Forbes-Leith had joined the Met in 1936 under the Trenchard scheme, an ultimately doomed attempt to introduce an officer class into the force. At Sandhurst military academy he'd won the belt of honour as the best cadet of his intake, and in the war was a captain in the Desert Rats and took part in the Normandy invasion. Afterwards he returned to the police, moving from the uniformed branch to CID in 1946, and rising meteorically through the ranks.

It was at the Old Bailey in 1954 that Forbes-Leith first came to national attention. The Lord Chief Justice Lord Goddard declared that the country was indebted to him for his work on "one of the most complicated and difficult cases I have come across since I have been a judge." It concerned Mrs Dorothy Lewis, a 51-year-old widow whose husband, a doctor, had placed his money in building societies in the names of his four daughters. When Dr Lewis died bankrupt and intestate, Mrs Lewis forged his will, transferring all the savings from her daughters' accounts to her own. Forbes-Leith discovered that she'd fallen under the influence of a 61-year-old man called Napoleon Ryder. "My view," he told the court, "is that this was a perfectly happy family up to the doctor's death, and they had quite a lot of money. Everything was going perfectly smoothly until Ryder appeared on the scene and from then onwards Mrs Lewis became completely under his domination."

Following this success, Forbes-Leith became, at 38 years of age, the youngest officer ever appointed to the rank of Detective Superintendent by Scotland Yard, and was soon assigned a curious case in which the two main clues were a cowboy hat and a pair of yellow gloves.

The Minister of Wesley's Chapel in Islington, north London, was away and his wife Mrs Edith Spivey was asleep in the manse when an intruder broke in late one night. The prowler stole her jewellery, tied her up, pulled a pillow case over her head and assaulted her. Mrs Spivey's description of the attacker was vague, but she recalled that he wore yellow gloves, and a cowboy hat was found in another room. So who was lurking around Islington in such a strange get-up in the early hours? It didn't take Forbes-Leith long to find out. Forty cowboy hats had been given away at a birthday party at a nearby pub. One of the guests matched the Minister's wife's description. When he was traced, tucked away in Bernard Smeeth's drawers were some yellow gloves. Smeeth got five years for the crime.

Two years later Forbes-Leith was acclaimed for his key role in the biggest police corruption case of the decade. For almost nine years a clique of Brighton officers solicited bribes from back-street abortionists, brothel-runners, illegal club-owners and petty crooks. The Chief Constable of Brighton was among those accused. More than 200 people were interviewed by Forbes-Leith's team, and 64 witnesses stepped forward to give evidence for the prosecution. The case was considered so serious that the Solicitor General, Sir Harry Hylton-Foster QC, presented the charges at the preliminary hearing. Two officers were eventually sentenced to five years in jail. Their shameless greed had the public and media transfixed, and Forbes-Leith and his officers were commended for their work, which, according to one judge, was "very arduous and not only arduous but invidious, inquiring into the malpractices of fellow members of the police force. It has been done with efficiency and integrity."

A glowing profile of Forbes-Leith subsequently appeared in the *Daily Express*. "We must forget that we are going to investigate police officers and treat this as just another criminal inquiry," he'd told his men as they embarked on the investigation, the paper said, adding: "This was the unflinching approach of Forbes-Leith, the man they call 'the pride of Hendon Police College' for a job that had to be done." He was "rated one of the best-dressed men at the Yard", enjoyed "rugby, squash and walking", while his hobbies included "wine, food and decorating his flat".

Now, at 42, he'd taken up the reins at Harrow Road: the latest step on an apparently seamless path to an illustrious career. "I shall endeavour to look after the good citizens and sort out the bad ones," he told a reporter from the *Paddington Mercury* as he began.

Sunday May 17, 1959. At 1.15am, Sid Coomber's phone call roused Forbes-Leith from his bed. Even half-asleep the implications of white youths killing a black man in Notting Hill would have been plain.

He dressed and waited for a police car to pick him up outside his home on Devonshire Close, near Harley Street. Within an hour he was at Harrow Road, arriving at the same moment as Detective Inspector Ferguson Walker. A shrewd Scotsman with a heavy accent, Walker had been on duty for twenty-one hours and slept for just two the previous night. They exchanged a few words in the station yard and entered the main CID room, where DC Buchan was taking a statement from one of the Jamaican witnesses, then went into Forbes-Leith's office. A uniformed officer brought in three cups of tea and Forbes-Leith unlocked his cupboard, took out a new Book 40 - a red, hard-covered A4 police notebook with indexed pages - and told Walker to take rough notes as Coomber outlined what he knew so far. When Coomber finished, Walker telephoned for more CID officers while Forbes-Leith put in a call for a police photographer.

Then the three detectives and George Isaacs - who'd already returned to the crime scene with Coomber in a brief, unsuccessful hunt for the murder weapon and witnesses - made the short journey to the corner of Golborne Road and Southam Street. Directly opposite was the Earl of Warwick pub, beside them a derelict, boarded-up shop and the Bagwash Laundry, where washing was paid for by weight - 12lbs of clothes cleaned for 3 shillings and six pence - and just across the junction on Golborne Road, the railway bridge crossing the main line into Paddington Station, which lay two miles down the tracks.

Isaacs ran through what he'd seen. Foremost in his mind were the three youths coming away from the spot. But despite saying he'd had a good look at them as they walked by on the other side of the road, he was unable to give firm descriptions. Nor could the passengers he'd dropped off at 87 Southam Street, whom Forbes-Leith woke with a knock on the door, and who had been drinking, in any case. Lewis and Steele were similarly imprecise. And so were Joy Okine and her mother, whom the police interviewed the next day.

They returned to Harrow Road, where Isaacs finished giving a statement at around 3.45am. He was about to leave when Forbes-Leith asked him about the dead man's missing brown suede shoe. Isaacs searched his cab, but it wasn't there, so Coomber was ordered back to the murder spot to look for it. As he left the station, Isaacs reappeared with the shoe in his hand: he'd discovered it near the public police phone box, next to where one of the youths had leapt on Kelso's back.

Forbes-Leith and Walker drove to St Charles' Hospital with Ken Steele to inspect the victim's body, before returning to Harrow Road, where Detective Sergeant John Merry, who was attached to Scotland Yard's photographic branch C3, arrived an hour later.

"I have an unusual message to pass on Sir," Merry told Forbes-Leith, and explained that when he'd picked up his equipment at Scotland Yard's Victoria Embankment headquarters en route to Harrow Road, a reporter at the entrance had handed him a copy of the *Sunday Express*. "I was told to give it to you personally, and the man said, 'Don't forget my name.' But Sir, unfortunately I've forgotten it already."

Merry handed the newspaper to Forbes-Leith, who studied the 4am flash headline *Murder in Notting Hill*.

"Good heavens," he remarked. "It's the front page. That's quick work. They even mentioned the fact I was called out of bed. But they've missed one thing. They forgot to mention I went to the toilet before leaving for the office."

At 6am Forbes-Leith, Walker and Coomber were once more on the corner of Southam Street and Golborne Road, this time with Merry, who took pictures of the scene from various angles. Nearby two men sat watching them closely in a light blue Ford Prefect. They were journalists.

* * *

At around the same time, the police were drawing up at the north London house where Kelso's cousin James Christian and his wife Rose lived on the third floor, in a single room with a large radiogram and a gas cooker on the landing. The couple's six-month old son had been crying.

"James, a car's here with five policemen," said Rose, looking out of the window.

"Come and feed the baby," he told her.

A couple of minutes later, the front door bell rang. Then their landlady appeared and said that the police wanted to see them. James was still in his pyjamas when they came up.

"Mr Christian, do you have a relative by the name of Kelso Benjamin Cochrane?" one asked.

"Yes. We are two sister's children [cousins]. What happened?"

"He died at 1 o'clock this morning. He was stabbed in the chest by Teddy Boys."

"Who stabbed him? White men like you? I will batter their lips down."

The police returned at 9am to take James to identify Kelso. On the way he asked to stop at a newsagents'. He'd never smoked a cigarette in his life, not even the pretend, roll-up ones his friends would light when he was young. But he went inside the shop, bought two packs, and lit up in the car. Shortly afterwards, he fainted at the sight of his best friend's body.

Olivia Ellington had learned that her boyfriend was dead with a knock at the door just before dawn. In her statement she told DI Walker that she'd known Kelso for eight months and that their relationship was "happy and steady".

"I have never seen him the worse for drinking," she said. "He always drank in moderation."

On Sunday morning, she pulled her green coat over her trainee nurse's uniform and went to see James and Rose before her hospital shift. Kelso's friends were already there, drinking to his memory. James couldn't stop crying. "Even though me and Kelso were not brothers, I will remember him until the day I die," he said.

Later, the papers carried Olivia's quotes: "Kelso was a quiet man and so very kind...He was not a fighting man. He would normally go out of his way to avoid trouble. He knew very few people in the area. It is obvious he was picked on for the very simple reason he was coloured."

* * *

Throughout Sunday more than 50 anti-riot officers swept into the district with extra police dogs. Black Marias were stationed in strategic locations, uniformed police patrolled in pairs and radio cars cruised the streets. Civil servants briefed the Home Secretary Rab Butler on the situation with regular calls to his home at Stanstead Hall, Essex. Notting Hill remained subdued.

Monday May 18, 1959. Less than two miles as the crow flies from where Kelso was stabbed, the traditional Bank Holiday fair was taking place in patchy sunshine at Wormwood Scrubs, the flat parkland bordered by the bleak Victorian jail of the same name. The police were out in strength - making their presence felt among the coconut shies, lucky dips and merry-go-rounds. There were flashes of tension, but nothing more. "On several occasions only a tactful withdrawal by a coloured man prevented an incident," said *The Times*. "Both races mixed freely but when a coloured family and a white couple wanted the same dodgem car the attendant ordered the coloured people off the floor and they left quietly."

* * *

The murder inquiry had been underway less than 48 hours, but Forbes-Leith had already reached an important conclusion. "The stabbing has absolutely nothing to do with racial conflict," he told the press. "The motive could have been robbery."

The same line was being pushed by an 'unnamed senior Scotland Yard officer' in the *Daily Mirror*. "We are satisfied that it was the work of a group of about six anti-law white teenagers who had only one motive in view - robbery or attempted robbery of a man who was walking the streets in the Notting Hill district alone in the early hours of the morning," he said. "The fact that he happened to be coloured does not, in our view, come into the question."

The paper cited Kelso's dying words to Lewis and Steele - "They asked me for money but I told them I didn't have any" - adding that Kelso's wallet was empty, and there was "not a penny piece in any of his pockets", despite the fact that he earned £15 a week and had only been paid the day before. Forbes-Leith was satisfied that the teenage gang responsible were from outside the area. They were probably broke after a night of pub-crawling, and would have robbed anyone they came across. Kelso, his left hand encased in plaster, was easy prey. The article ended bluntly: "One or more of the teenage gang could face a charge of murder in the furtherance of robbery. The penalty for this is HANGING."

On the same day, Allan Morais, Deputy Commissioner of the West Indies, visited Harrow Road station and spoke to detectives. Afterwards he branded the idea that the crime wasn't racially motivated "complete and utter nonsense". "Mosleyite agitators are prodding youths into seeking fights with coloured people," he said.

Sir Oswald Mosley, scion of the land-owning aristocracy and prospective MP for North Kensington, was quick to seize upon Forbes-Leith's pronouncement. "On May 17 a negro was reported murdered in the Notting Hill district," he said. "The next day some daily papers suggested that this was due to racial tension and that I was responsible on account of my prospective candidature, although I had just circulated to every house in the area to settle the question by 'votes not violence'... Leading Conservatives were even quoted as having suggested that I should in future be held responsible for any repetition of troubles which had occurred before I even arrived. The same evening the police brought this particular nonsense to an end by stating the motive for the murder appeared to be ordinary robbery. The only cure for these troubles is to send the Jamaicans back to a fair deal in their own country by restoring the prosperity of their sugar industry."

* * *

To solve the crime, Forbes-Leith had 24 officers at his disposal. He split them into three groups. The first began locating and interviewing young men with criminal records in the area, relying on local intelligence as well as Scotland Yard's central index system, which catalogued every convicted criminal in the country. Soon, dozens of youths were passing through Harrow Road for questioning. The second group searched for the murder weapon. The third started house-to-house enquiries in the vicinity of the crime scene, working their way along Golborne

Road and Southam Street.

The roads lay within Golborne Ward. According to the most recent census it was the most overcrowded district in London, with a population density five times greater than the capital's average. Southam Street's narrow, terraced houses reeked of decades of decay. There were rotten window frames, peeling plasterwork and doors boarded with corrugated iron. Trains rattled down the tracks which ran parallel, and a hulking gasworks loomed at the back. The police soon learned of the parties that had taken place in the neighbourhood on Saturday night.

Two hundred yards from where Kelso fell, the passage inside 18 Southam Street was lined with crates of empty beer bottles: the dregs of an all-night drinking session. Invites had been handed out at local pubs through the evening, and just before closing time people dipped in their pockets for a whip-round, and then carried bottles over to the house. "I hold a party every weekend for the local lads," said the host, Ma O'Brien, a costermonger's widow. "They are as good as gold. This murder disgusts me." Police interviewed the guests about what they'd seen.

Another party also entered Forbes-Leith's radar. Upstairs at The Mitre pub on Golborne Road, guests marked a young couple's wedding with a reception lasting from early Saturday afternoon to late that evening. One incident in particular aroused Forbes-Leith's suspicions. At first sight, it appeared potentially significant.

As midnight approached and the celebration was in its last throes, seven youths lingered, drinking what was left on the tables. They'd arrived near the end and were reluctant to leave. After a little persuasion - and the offer of a couple of bottles of beer each - they relented.

Around half an hour later, a black man left another party in Hazelwood Crescent, near the top of Golborne Road. He walked towards the railway bridge, oblivious as he passed the junction with Southam Street that Kelso had lain dying there not long before. He noticed nothing unusual and saw nobody. Fifty yards on, the white youths who'd just been asked to leave The Mitre were loitering on the pavement opposite. As the black man drew level, one lobbed a beer bottle over the road at him, and then the group crossed over and started hurling abuse. But just at that moment more people from the Hazelwood Crescent party arrived, and after a short confrontation the youths sloped off towards Portobello Road.

The police traced the gang, who numbered seven in total and were aged between 17 and 22. They conveniently omitted any mention of the bottle-throwing incident at first, but in a second interview were confronted with evidence, and admitted it. Yet, in the end, Forbes-Leith concluded that they couldn't have attacked Kelso Cochrane, since they were apparently still in The Mitre at the crucial time.

The second group of detectives was busy searching for the knife in North Kensington's grimy nooks and corners. They foraged in old bomb sites, sifted through rubbish dumps, dug around slum basements. A children's paddling pond was scoured and an ornamental pond drained. They trundled up and down the main line into Paddington, and with council workmen, excavated 30 drains in five streets around the murder spot. What emerged would have provided a future anthropologist with enough evidence to draw a vivid portrait of the area's street life: a razor, a bicycle chain, several coshes, lengths of iron piping, milk bottles with their tops knocked off (ready to use in street fights), and a knife (but not the one they were after).

The police also looked into Kelso's past for clues that might lead them to his killer. It was discovered that he had no known enemies in the district, and the possibility that his death was the result of a reprisal was therefore dismissed.

Scotland Yard dismiss a racial motive to the crime.

Copyright: Mirrorpix.

The Notting Hill Squad

Tuesday May 19, 1959. The number of people on the killer's trail was growing. Now it wasn't only the police who were after him, but some self-styled sleuths who'd attended Ma O'Brien's celebration in Southam Street. Under the headline, *The posse in tight trousers hunts a killer*, the *Daily Express* explained how:

"Five young men set out last night to find the Notting Hill killer. They had all been questioned by police at Harrow Road police station. And 12 of their friends joined them to find out who stabbed 32-year-old West Indian Kelso Cochrane on Whit Sunday. The young men - in tight trousers, pointed shoes and slicked down hair - began to comb out the score of clubs in the streets of crumbling houses within half a mile of the murder corner on Southam Street.

They went around in little groups and conducted the search in whispers over glasses of beer in the dingy club rooms where juke boxes played harshly, lights burned softly and girls in flared skirts jived.

One of the self-appointed 'Notting Hill Squad', 22-year-old Peter Bell of Talbot Grove, said: 'We are not doing this for the sake of the police. Two of our mates are still at the police station. The police say this could be a hanging job and we don't want any suspicion attached to any of us.'

Lean, dark-haired Bell - married with one child - left the police station at midnight on Monday. He was there for six hours. He said: 'We may not be angels round here, but we don't stand for knifing. So we are going to put ourselves around and make it our business to dig this one out.'" Helping him in his quest, said the *Kensington Post*, who also reported this development, were his brother Mark Bell and friends George Baker and Brian Donaghue.

Bell's picture in the *Daily Express* showed a young man in a jacket and tie who had an easy smile, swept-back hair and slightly protruding ears. The two friends still being questioned were 20-year-old Pat Digby, a tall, blonde painter who had worked as a steward in the Merchant Navy, and his shorter companion Shoggy Breagan, a 24-year-old labourer. They'd been detained for questioning for more than 24 hours, and had their meals brought to them from the police canteen. Detectives had visited their homes in Notting Dale, collecting a tweed coat, a shirt and pair of grey trousers from Digby's, and blue jeans and a black pullover from Breagan's.

Wednesday May 20, 1959. It was a day of frantic activity at Harrow Road. Six police cars brought seven men and four women to the station for questioning. They included two women, one holding a baby; a black man and a white woman; and a man who crouched on the back seat covering his face with a rolled-up newspaper as he entered. All eleven were later allowed to leave. So were Pat Digby and Shoggy Breagan. That evening, after around 50 hours in custody, they went home.

Residents stared out of their windows into the fading light, as Breagan, wearing a pale pearl-grey suit and blue shirt, arrived back in Wilsham Street escorted by Forbes-Leith. His mum Edith hugged him and the detective looked away. Shoggy's dad had died in 1954, but the rest of his family - from his 74-year-old gran to his seven siblings - gathered in the small front room where plastic ducks and fading photos hung on the walls. His five-year-old brother leapt on his lap, and his mother kept on reassuring him: "It doesn't matter," she said. "It doesn't matter."

Sipping a glass of ale, the young man relived his two days of captivity for reporters. He'd been questioned twice, he said. "I'll never forget this as long as I live. I kept telling the police I knew nothing about it. But they seemed to think I could tell them who did it. I told them I'd been to a party with Digby and we came out and saw this coloured bloke lying on the pavement. I said to Digby: 'It's nothing to do with us. Leave him alone.' We thought he was drunk. At 8pm, Breagan had been told he could go. "A copper said: 'We have nothing we can hold you on. You're being released for the time being.' All I want to do is forget I was in there."

He went on. "I can't understand why they suspected me. Most of the time they left me alone in my cell. The suspense was terrible. When I was alone I couldn't help thinking that it might be my lot and I'd end up being topped...Marwood, the thought of what happened to Marwood kept running through my head."

Twelve days before, a young scaffolder from Islington called Ron Marwood had gone to the gallows for fatally stabbing a policeman outside a dancehall.

A similar scene was unfolding 150 yards away on Princedale Road, where Pat Digby's mum Emily and his sister Rose waited on the doorstep to welcome him home. Emily, who was widowed, had grey hair tied in a bun, and steadied herself with a walking stick. She'd been crying. Rose, a slim girl in a thick blue coat, had sat for three hours at the station while her brother was being held, but the police hadn't let her see him. His friends in Talbot Grove had a celebration planned, but Digby, dressed in blue jeans and a blue shirt, wanted to go straight home, where a cup of tea awaited him. Cries of "Good luck Pat" echoed among the neighbours. A reporter began questioning him. "Let's forget it," he said. "I've been talking all this time trying to help."

Digby soon relented, and was quoted in the following day's paper. "It's the worst experience I've ever gone through," he said. He'd been questioned in an upstairs room at Harrow Road, and had told the police: "I had an argument with Shoggy Breagan. We went outside. We were on the point of having a fight in the street when we decided that maybe a walk would cool us down. As we turned into Golborne Road five chaps passed us. One of them was wearing a cap. We had never seen any of them before. Fifty yards up the road we had sorted out our little argument and turned to go back to the party. When we reached the corner we saw this black man lying on the pavement, clutching his chest. Two Spades - that's what we call coloured men here - were standing beside him. We decided to get out of it fast. It was not our business. Then when we saw how serious it was we decided to come clean and tell the lot. I had a lot of bloodstains on my clothes. For that matter all my clothes have blood on them. You know, from one fight or another. Old stuff. We fight a lot here. Life is like that in Notting Hill. The police took away all my clothes but I was in the clear."

The next day, said the *Daily Express*, Breagan took his girlfriend to a film matinee, while Digby sought the advice of George Rogers, the Labour MP for North Kensington. On Friday they met at Roger's Ladbroke Grove office. With Digby were three friends, who had also been questioned about the murder.

While Digby spoke with the MP in his room they waited outside, and fell into an argument with Olive Wilson, the local London County Councillor. She asked them why they didn't work and they swore at her. "We're not going to get jobs earning £6 a week," said one. "That's alright for the spades. I've been drawing £5 a week from the National Assistance for ten months. It's up to Mr Rogers to get us decent jobs."

George Rogers wouldn't disclose details of his conversation with Digby.

Sunday May 24, 1959. A 'Keep Britain White' banner stretched between the lions at the foot of Nelson's Column. Around 2,000 people - many of them students who had come to heckle - were at Trafalgar Square for the 'Keep Britain White' rally. The first speaker was greeted with a cry of "Who killed Kelso Cochrane?" Boos, mocking Nazi-style salutes, cries of "Seig Heil" and "No colour bar in Britain", continued through the meeting. The loudest jeers however, were reserved for Colin Jordan, whose White Defence League had organised the event with another far-right group, the National Labour Party. In his speech Jordan said black immigrants were "riddled with infectious diseases" including leprosy, and described Kelso Cochrane as a "manufactured martyr".

Monday May 25, 1959. The Duke of Edinburgh's visit had been arranged months ago, the Buckingham Palace spokesman stressed. "It is purely fortuitous that it comes after certain other events in that area."

Inside the Rugby Club - founded "to benefit the poor of Notting Dale" in 1884 - the Duke watched young girls jive to 'pop' records. "You're not going at it nearly hard enough," he said, before asking a boy what games he played.

"Cricket and soccer, but I am thinking of taking up polo if I can get some horses."

"Why not try bicycle polo?" he suggested. "That's good fun."

Five Rugby Club members were exiled from all this excitement. They'd been interrogated at Harrow Road about the murder and were therefore barred from attending. They waited sullenly on the bomb site outside among the large crowd of mostly women and children.

"I was questioned by the police but I had nothing to do with the murder. I'd like to be in the club but they won't have me. There's nothing else to do around here except hate the coloured boys," said one. "The police kept me for over two hours," added his friend. "If we could go in the club we won't get in trouble on the streets."

When the Duke emerged, the crowd cheered and surged. They patted his back and someone touched his collar. The Royal car pulled away, people put their hands to its windows, as the police formed a chain to clear an exit route. The five young men walked to the corner of the road and stood in silence by a shop.

That same afternoon, a mile or so north on the narrow crossing of Carlton Bridge, a much smaller gathering of spectators and journalists watched as three officers in a barge dragged a huge magnet through the dank waters of the Grand Union Canal, scraping the sludge at the bottom like fishermen trawling the seabed. They were five hundred yards from the corner of Southam Street and Golborne Road, the nearest point in the canal to the murder spot. The operation had been insti-gated after a tip-off. The rusting remnants of a pram were dredged up and passed to detectives on the bank. Then came a car lamp, tin cans, odd pieces of metal and some bike handlebars. The barge crossed back and forth before the shadows lengthened, the sky turned gloomy and the search for the knife ended in vain.

* * *

Silence is the code

Pessimism was starting to creep into the investigation, even though it had only been going a week. The mood was captured on the front-page of the *Kensington News*: *"Up to the time of going to press the usually noisy streets of 'Notting Hill', the new, erroneous, but notorious name for any part of North Kensington where there is trouble, have kept their secret and the police, despite intensive house-to-house inquiries, have failed, in the face of a wall of silence, to trace the killer of Kelso Cochrane...Notting Hill has closed its eyes and ears to this crime. The woman who told a policeman that a boy he sought 'lived up a tree' was typical of hundreds who have been taught to keep out of trouble...The statement by the police that they are convinced that the murder has no racial significance has been received with apathy by both the coloured and the white people. They believe in the wisdom of the statement but not its truth...Against this background a new, more subtle element has moved into the uneasy atmosphere of these teeming streets where over 10,000 coloured people are believed to live. It is the whisper growing in volume - that the law has failed in its duty to protect the coloured man, and that he must make his own protection or allow others to do it for him."*

Locals' innate reluctance to talk to the police was only part of it: some feared reprisals. "The gangs round here would take revenge on any white person they thought had given information," an unnamed white youth told a reporter.

The officer on 24-hour guard outside the Golborne Road house where Joy Okine and her mum had seen the attack from their first-floor flat, showed this was a prospect the police took seriously. Self-preservation was also why the author of a letter that found its way to Harrow Road chose to remain anonymous. "There is a mother in Golborne Road who has restrained her daughter from telling the police what she knows," it read. "The daughter can identify the two men responsible." The letter was of little evidential worth to the police, however, who said that they believed ten witnesses to the killing had still to come forward.

Among them were the two young men who approached Ken Steele and Horatio Lewis as they aided the stricken Kelso, and who offered to go after the attackers. They were described as being in their early twenties: one slim, fair and around 5ft 8in; the other possibly ginger, around 5ft 6in and wearing a light sports jacket.

By now the police were positing a new theory. It ran like this: two groups of youths were in the vicinity when the stabbing occurred; one stopped Cochrane, demanded money and attacked him; the other saw the affray and joined in; they all sprinted off when they realised the black man had been knifed.

Friday May 29, 1959. A parcel with a London postmark arrived at Harrow Road addressed to Det Supt Forbes-Leith. Inside was a five-inch bone-handled knife with a single blade. Could it be the murder weapon? In the expert opinion of Home Office pathologist Dr Donald Teare, the answer was no. Somebody was wasting the police's time.

Sunday May 31, 1959. After fifteen days, a breakthrough had come - or so it must have appeared to readers of the *Sunday Pictorial*. The newspaper seemed to confirm what many were saying: this really was a political killing. Fascists hadn't simply inflamed feelings in Notting Hill. They had planned and executed a black man's death there.

Following "days in hiding", Gordon Lewis, a "haggard and hungry" 19-year-old from north London, had broken cover.

"The murder of Kelso Cochrane was a diabolical publicity stunt that went wrong," he told journalist Tom Mangold. Lewis claimed he'd been asked to help beat up a black man, but it had escalated into murder. The plot had been hatched several weeks before at a meeting of the "undercover direct action committee" of one of the far-right groups operating in the district. "It decided to organise the roughing up of six coloured people in Notting Hill. The idea was to attract publicity for their meetings." Lewis explained: "A former political friend of mine was chosen as the go-between to get professional thugs to inflict the beatings. I was told to be his assistant. He said I could earn money for this. I didn't know that Cochrane was to be a victim or that it was to be a murder. But I don't like blood money, so I ducked out." They were paid more than £200 and the go-between had now left the country, the paper reported, adding that Lewis had passed this information on to Forbes-Leith.

In truth, the young man's claims wilted under scrutiny.

The police found that *"he had no facts to back up his allegation"*, and when Special Branch investigated, they concluded that the newspaper may have been the target of a sting. *"Enquiries revealed that Lewis lived next door to and was very friendly with Benjamin Franklyn Levene"* said a Special Branch report. *"Levene has come to notice on numerous occasions as a hoaxer, whose modus operandi is to tell the press sensational but false stories in the hope of payment. Lewis was interviewed and made a written confession that his statements to the Sunday Pictorial were completely false."*

CHAPTER THREE

BACKSTAGE MANOEUVRES

Friday June 5, 1959. In an opulent Whitehall building decorated with oil paintings of figures from Britain's imperial past, a group of officials gathered to discuss the Cochrane case and the situation in Notting Hill.

In attendance were Lord Perth, Minister of State for Colonial Affairs, and a man with patrician charm and an unflappable manner; Philip Rogers, one of the leading civil servants of the day, renowned for his ability to elegantly distil complex arguments; and, along with two other Colonial Office representatives and one from the Home Office, a troop of leading West Indian politicians - the Barbadian QC and Prime Minister of the Federation of the West Indies, Grantley Adams; his deputy Dr Carl La Corbiniere; and Garnet Gordon CBE, Commissioner in the United Kingdom for the West Indies, whose primary duty was overseeing the welfare of his compatriots in the UK.

The meeting was held in Lord Perth's room at the Colonial Office, and was confidential. It was agreed that no statement would be given to the press, though if asked, according to the minutes: *"the representatives of the West Indies would say that they had paid a courtesy call on the Minister of State, during which a number of subjects of mutual interest were discussed."*

Lord Perth said that Notting Hill *"was a particularly difficult area"* and that the number of police there was to be increased. Then they moved on to the matter of immediate concern: Kelso Cochrane's funeral service, due to take place the following day.

The police were doing everything possible to ensure nothing untoward happened, said Philip Rogers. Garnet Gordon was nevertheless worried that the arrangements *"were now in the hands of an African organisation that would exploit the funeral"*. He meant the Inter-Racial Friendship Co-ordinating Council, founded in the wake of Kelso's murder by activists including Claudia Jones, the chain-smoking communist editor of the *West Indian Gazette*. Jones and the Council had helped raise the £257 cost of the funeral, and were pushing for laws against incitement to racial hatred.

Dr La Corbiniere added his concerns. *"Strong political influences were now at work on both sides...which were laying the foundation of future trouble,"* he said. He had a solution: moving Kelso's body out of England: *"There was a danger of emotional pilgrimages to the grave, and at some future stage Mr Cochrane's parents should be asked if they wanted the remains transferred to Trinidad [where Kelso's father was living]."*

The idea was left hanging, although it was decided that if the body was to be repatriated: *"it would be wise to allow a reasonable interval of time to elapse, so that interest in the case might have died down, and the removal effected without undue publicity."*

There was consensus on Claudia Jones and her fellow activists. *"It was generally agreed that the West Indian members should dissociate themselves from the activities of the Council. It was, however, essential to time this action carefully if the Council was to be discredited."* With that settled, the following day the three West Indian dignitaries joined the throng at Kelso's funeral, alongside the events' organisers whose reputations they wished to tarnish.

Saturday June 13, 1959. A week after Kelso's burial, a well-spoken maths teacher from Coventry was seen on the streets of Notting Hill advancing a bizarre theory about the murder. Special Branch spotted Colin Jordan handing out leaflets which asked the question hecklers had shouted at his Keep Britain White rally three weeks before: *"Who Killed Kelso Cochrane?"* The answer, the leaflets suggested, was a conspiracy involving Jews and communists, whose motive was to smear groups like his and get anti-discrimination laws passed:

"The people behind the coloured invasion are getting desperate because of the growing white resistance in Notting Hill. Reds are forming strong-arm squads in support of the blacks. Jews have threatened to destroy the premises of the White Defence League. Now they are using the killing of a coloured man to:

Smear the white folk of Notting Hill.

Frame white resistance organisations in the district.

Demand new laws to stifle and punish resistance.

Was Cochrane's killing arranged for this foul purpose?

We stand for the white people of Notting Hill against the coloured invasion."

Notting Hill's white working-class appeared less interested in standing by the Cambridge graduate with a taste in jackboots and Nazi regalia, than Special Branch were. The latter kept surveillance on the White Defence League's Princedale Road HQ at the weekends, when Jordan travelled down from Coventry to open it. Despite widespread publicity, they noted in a memo, that *"no private meetings appear to have been held there and very little local interest has been shown in the premises."*

Jordan's little band of aspiring race warriors weren't Special Branch's sole preoccupation in the neighbourhood. The police's intelligence-gathering arm on domestic subversion was also keeping tabs on Notting Hill's left-wing groups, whom they identified as being partly responsible for the deteriorating relationship between black people and the police:

"A 'whispering campaign' of police brutality has been conducted in the Notting Hill area for the past two or three months," read a confidential report. *"Rumours of beatings up in police cells, of coloured men being detained for hours in the police station and not being charged, and of heads being flushed in WC pans have abounded galore. None of the complaints has had any foundation of truth...It is difficult to determine the source of these rumours. They could be the work of malicious gossipers but such rumours suit the policy of the extreme left-wing parties which are now actively opposing fascism in these*

districts... *The extreme left-wing has found a fertile field for propaganda amongst the coloured people who are being exploited to further Communist and Trotskyist aims..."*

Special Branch also logged the comments of an activist called Muzaffa Alijah at a meeting of the Coloured Workers' Welfare Association in Hyde Park: *"[Alijah] accused Mosley of being responsible for the murder of Kelso Cochrane and of inciting the white people against the black. Alijah said that police investigating the murder of Cochrane had asked for the co-operation of the coloured people but, he maintained, this was an insult to the intelligence of the black man, because the same police had been arresting coloured people daily and taking them to Harrow Road police station, where they were beaten up. He contended that Cochrane's murderer could be arrested at once, but in this country there was police protection only for those who had property. Black people had no property and, therefore, they went without protection."*

A knife-wielding Teddy Boy is urged on by a Nazi - political cartoonist Ken Sprague's take on the murder.
Reproduced with kind permission of the Ken Sprague Fund.

A meeting on 'murder corner'

The weeks slipped by, the country basked in sustained sunshine, and Cliff Richard and The Drifters' *Living Doll* seemed permanently lodged at number one in the pop charts. In a corner of west London, Sir Oswald Mosley's campaign to represent the people of North Kensington in parliament was gathering pace.

Tuesday July 21, 1959. Children darted in and out of the crowd as women shouted the news to one another from their windows: "Mosley's coming". Of all the places in North Kensington for the Union Movement to hold a public rally on a balmy evening, none held the significance of the junction of Golborne Road and Southam Street.

At the front stood his supporters, mostly serious-faced men in their twenties and thirties. Further back from the crowd of about 300 were the curious: students, black people, workmen, housewives. The *North Kensington Leader* was passed around, and then cheers sounded as Mosley stepped up to the platform. The sociologist Ruth Glass was there, and later described the scene:

"He points to the forgotten people of North Kensington, to their miserable housing conditions, to 'the years of Tory-Labour neglect' and to the coloured invasion, which are, he says, responsible for all this hopelessness. The solution: 'Fight to the end the coloured invasion. Send the Jamaicans home.'"

Applause rang out, Sir Oswald stepped down and the meeting ended. *"But is it really over? Everybody expects a sequel. The crowds drift along, and then bunch up again, waiting. After all, this is the Cochrane corner. The police come: 'Break it up.'...An open loudspeaker lorry, packed with Mosley's cadets, comes along; shouts go to and fro. Suddenly the coloured people no longer walk singly...Only one Negro is still on his own: standing a few steps away on the railway bridge, in a melancholy posture of wait and see..."*

Thursday October 8, 1959. Three months later, Sir Oswald Mosley was roundly defeated at the ballot box. For the first time in his political life - since entering the House of Commons as Tory MP for Harrow as a mere 22-year-old in 1918 - he lost his deposit: coming last in the battle to represent the people of North Kensington with 2,821 votes.

* * *

Throughout the early months of summer, Forbes-Leith's team had ploughed on: knocking on doors and chasing leads, fanning out north beyond Golborne Road and Southam Street, and spreading their enquiries further west, to Hammersmith and Shepherd's Bush, where they traced the movements of gang members known to hang around Notting Hill. In all, they took 905 statements. Of these, only nine threw up any fresh information.

At around midnight that Saturday, for example, one person saw a group of white youths aged about 15 or 16 on the corner of the road opposite the Bagwash Laundry arguing about where to go. The witness saw a black man - Kelso Cochrane - walk down Southam Street, pass a lamp post on the left hand side, and head towards the corner as if to turn into Golborne Road, at which point he walked into the youths. One youth spoke and a scuffle started.

A second witness looked out of their window after hearing a disturbance and saw a man, aged around 30, racing down Golborne Road towards Southam Street. A woman was running behind him. She wore a skirt, a cardigan and an apron, and had her hair tied in a scarf in a turban fashion. The woman was then seen crossing Southam Street with a different man. Shortly afterwards, a black man - Kelso Cochrane - was sitting in the road by the kerb being helped by two other black men - Horatio Lewis and Ken Steele. At that precise moment, the man the witness had seen running down Golborne Road before, passed a few feet by them with another man, and disappeared down Southam Street.

The significance of the running couple and that they were each seen with different men wasn't clear.

A third witness saw five youths hanging around the Bagwash Laundry. They surrounded a black man, first talking, then pushing and shoving him. The black man fell to the ground. Next, two other youths arrived and spoke to the two black men helping the victim: Lewis and Steele. The witness was unable to say whether these two youths were part of the original five.

A fourth witness heard shouting from the direction of the corner of Golborne Road soon after midnight. It sounded like there was going to be a fight, and a woman was yelling "Stop".

Some thirty minutes later, another witness recounted, four youths, one of them about 20, the rest aged 16 or 17, made their way furtively down Southam Street. The older one was telling the others: "Don't keep looking back." They turned up Golborne Road towards Kensal Road.

More fragments emerged. A girl came forward after overhearing two men talking about the murder in a Notting Hill club, which according to the *News Chronicle* "gave a clue as to who might have stabbed Kelso Cochrane". She was offered police protection. Others - all wanting guarantees that their identities would be protected - gave names or scraps of information. But nothing, according to Forbes-Leith, amounted to hard evidence. And none of the eyewitnesses could identify the assailants - just as George Isaacs, Joy Okine, her mother, Steele and Lewis had been unable to - despite being shown the photos of possible suspects.

In July Forbes-Leith submitted an interim report to the Met's Assistant Commissioner. By then, the murder investigation was inevitably being scaled back.

* * *

Monday October 19, 1959. Notting Hill's relative calm was threatened by a single shot in the dead of night. A 29-year-old Dominican by the name of Dill Simon was restless after drinking coffee, so he went out for a breath of fresh air and ran into his friend, Frederick Burrs. At 3am they strolled down Talbot Road, in the heart of the Colville district. Reaching the junction of Powis Gardens, five white men and two white girls stopped and asked them the way to a club, which they didn't know. As Simon and Burrs wandered off, they glanced back to see one of the white men struggling with one of the girls: he was trying to grab a pistol out of her handbag, and she was trying to resist him. The black men ran, but a bullet caught Simon's right wrist. The gunman was about 24-years-old, tall, with blonde hair showing from under an Alpine-style trilby.

The Daily Worker asked: *"Are Kelso's Killers on the move again?"*, but Special Branch noted that: *"Unlike the Cochrane affair, no special coverage was given to [the shooting], and on the facts available the incident does not appear to have any racial bearing"*.

Simon was interviewed by the *West Indian Gazette*. "I know the police do not believe me, but a white man fired at me because I'm coloured," he said. The shooting may have happened exactly as he described, but Dill Joseph Simon proved an unreliable witness. On September 19 1963, he received a life sentence for battering and strangling Elizabeth (Gwen) Davies to death at her home in Powis Square, W11, in what he claimed was an argument over money.

* * *

Friday February 26, 1960. The murder inquiry had wound down, but the question of what to do with Kelso's body - raised in Whitehall the day before his funeral - rumbled on for months behind the scenes in letters between the Home Office, the Colonial Office and West Indian officials.

On the one hand, officials feared that *"mischief makers"* would use his grave in London *"to spark trouble"*. On the other, they worried that if his body was repatriated to the West Indies, it was *"practically certain that the arrival… would be used as an occasion for demonstrations on a considerable scale which would arouse fears and inflame animosities"*. In the end, removing it was considered the greater risk, *"from a broad public point of view"*. So Kelso's remains were left undisturbed.

Nine months after his death, the authorities' fears had proved unfounded: far from becoming a political shrine, the burial plot near the front of Kensal Green Cemetery where hundreds had packed in emotional scenes the previous summer, lay abandoned, as the *Kensington News* reported:

"A forgotten, neglected grave at the foot of a blackened, dead plane tree in Kensal Green Cemetery, with a wooden tag stamped 54504 marks the resting place of Kelso Cochrane, who, by his murder became the martyr of Notting Hill… The brutal murder of this quiet citizen shocked the whole nation… But no headstone marks his grave. No flowers bloom to perpetuate his memory. Nothing but brown earth and a wooden tag…'The promise has still not been fulfilled that Kelso Cochrane would be remembered with full honours,' said a spokesman of the Coloured People's Progressive Association this week. 'It's an absolute scandal. I've really been hurt about this.'"

One man who read the article was particularly shocked. His name was Randolph Beresford, and like Kelso, he was a West Indian-born carpenter who lived in west London. Beresford put down the newspaper, turned to his wife, and said: "I'm going to start a memorial fund for this young man." The cost of a headstone was £16: the same as a tailor-made suit from Burton's, he calculated. After approaching the local Trades Council for help, he had soon raised enough for a Portland stone slab, which was unveiled at a little memorial service at Kensal Green. "I am not doing this as a West Indian," he told the *Kensington News*. "Please make that clear. It is not a colour question, just the feeling of one human being for another. After all, it might have been any one of us who fell victim to the murderer's knife that night."

Friday June 3, 1960. More than a year had passed since the murder, and whatever the killer was feeling - denial, a lingering fear of being betrayed, twisted self-righteousness, who knows, maybe even a flicker of remorse - if he happened to read all the way to the bottom of that day's *Kensington News* front page article headlined *Cochrane Killer Is Still Free*, he might have felt a surge of relief, and a growing certainty he had got away with it.

"Millions of people will be setting out by road and rail for their Whitsun holiday. This beginning of the summer Bank Holiday is the cue for an assault on the beaches of England...Many of them will be travelling by car. Last year 73 people were killed in accidents on the roads. But in fact 74 were killed over last Whitsun. The seventy-fourth was not killed by a car. He was killed by a knife through the heart in a backstreet of Notting Hill...The silent streets of Notting Hill refuse to yield up the secrets of Kelso's killing. Police investigations still go on under the direction of Detective Superintendent Ian Forbes-Leith at Harrow Road police station. But a local police officer is reported to have said during an informal discussion six months ago: 'We know who killed Kelso Cochrane - but we can't prove it.' If this is true then the question must be asked: 'If the police cannot prove it now, will they ever be able to prove it?' Barring a confession from the killer it seems unlikely...[The police] have worked long and hard on this case. Their task has been monumental. Should Kelso's killer never be found no fault will be found with the police..."

It would be fifteen months before the murder returned to the headlines. This time it wasn't a policeman who claimed to know the killer's identity, but one of Oswald Mosley's most rabid followers.

* * *

A Great Patriot

In the league of swivel-eyed supremacists agitating in the late 50s and early 60s, Peter Dawson was a match even for the outlandish Colin Jordan. With sunken cheeks and receding hair, the circulation manager for the Union Movement's *Action* newsletter pursued his dreams of racial purity with obsessive zeal.

A brief run through his record from the end of 1959 to the middle of 1961 finds him:

Painting three large swastikas and *Juden Raus* on the synagogue opposite the Union Movement's office on Kensington Park Road, W11.

Set off a home-made bomb outside the same UM office ten days later. (He was trying to frame a Jewish group.)

Organise a protest against the marriage of the black Jewish Sammy Davis Jnr and the white Swedish actress Mai Britt outside the Pigalle restaurant in the West End, (where Davis was performing in a cabaret).

Disrupt a meeting calling for the boycott of South African goods (for which he was fined £20).

Send fascist literature as a wedding present to Princess Margaret and Anthony Armstrong-Jones.

Appear at the Old Bailey charged with breaking in and setting fire to the anti-apartheid movement's Bloomsbury headquarters (he was acquitted).

Dawson even managed to provoke a minor diplomatic incident. On the evening of July 23 1960, he approached a police officer outside The Ritz Hotel, and informed him: "We are going to do a bit of peaceful picketing for the departure of the Prime Minister of Congo." He was brandishing a megaphone and accompanied by colleagues with banners stating: "*Mosley says stand by White Africa*", "*Rapers of Children go home*" and "*Bongo, bongo, bongo, whites aren't going to leave the Congo*". They were protesting against the presence of Patrice Lumumba, the first democratically elected black leader of the newly independent Congo and a hero for anti-colonialists, who was resting at the hotel during a stop-over in London.

During his short stay at The Ritz, Lumumba was visited by Ghana's High Commissioner, Sir Edward Asafu-Adjaye. When the Commissioner descended the hotel steps afterwards, Dawson struck, punching him in the face, knocking him down, and screaming: "Black savages. We'll smash you back to the jungle". He'd mistaken the Ghanaian diplomat for the Congolese Prime Minister. Dawson was still ranting as the police carted him off, and was later sentenced to three months in jail for the attack.

John Profumo, Minister of State for Foreign Affairs, called Asafu-Adjaye to convey his sorrow at the incident and a statement was made in parliament expressing the profound hope that relations between the two countries wouldn't be damaged. Even Mosley sought to distance himself from his devotee:

"We must avoid giving the effect of being cracked or childish...we must consider whether our activities attract people to our cause or repel them," he wrote. Dawson was eventually expelled from the Union Movement and wrote to Horace Sherman Miller, head of the Ku Klux Klan in America, offering his services.

Then came his claims about Kelso Cochrane.

September 1961. Ken Gardner of *The People* interviewed the sometime ice-cream salesman and van driver in his "dingy" second-floor tenement flat in Shoreditch, east London. *"Britain's No 1 Jew-baiter, negro-persecutor and mischief maker in chief",* who had *"carried out a campaign of terror, hate and bullying which it is hard to believe could happen in modern-day Britain,"* told Gardner: *"I hate Jews and blacks and I'm prepared to spend the rest of my life getting them out of this country".*

Dawson, who had lived in Notting Hill after the riots and been a UM party organiser for west London, bragged that he knew the name of Kelso Cochrane's killer: *"It was one of the Union mob. A great guy. Did it to teach the nigs a lesson. But none of us in the Movement would tell the police a thing."*

The next week he sought to make a correction, of sorts, in a letter to the paper:

"In Ken Gardner's attack on me ("The Biggest Bully in Britain is Unmasked") he says rightly that I know the name of Kelso Cochrane's killer. But he is wrong when he calls Cochrane a 'worker'. In fact he was a gangster of the worst possible type - deported from America for criminal activities and carrying on a profession as a dope peddler when he arrived in Great Britain. The facts are: he pulled a knife on a friend of mine, my friend disarmed him and in the process Cochrane stabbed himself." Peter Dawson, London E1

Thursday October 12, 1961. As a result of the newspaper articles Dawson was interviewed by the police. They placed no reliance on his claims.

* * *

May 2009. On one side of the motorway was a shopping centre where old East End exiles were going about their business alongside brightly dressed West Africans and Asian women in hijabs. On the other side, was a low-rise estate where a young lady pushed a pram, speaking into her mobile as she walked across the freshly mowed lawn. An empty packet of Mayfair cigarettes and a discarded takeaway box ('Sam's - the home of great tasting chicken'), were the only litter on the otherwise unblemished landscape.

This Essex outpost - a warren of little closes and cul-de-sacs radiating suburban order - was where Peter Dawson had washed up. It was almost half a century since he'd been at the vanguard of the fight to rid Britain of *'undesirable foreign elements'*. But as a card-carrying member of the British National Party he was still wedded to the far-right, albeit as a pensioner paying reduced subs.

The upstairs double-glazed window was slightly open. It appeared someone was home. A woman with dyed blonde hair came to the door.

"Is Peter Dawson here?"

"He's my husband." She looked about 50, young enough to be his daughter.

I explained why I wanted to speak to him. I'd already sent a letter and knocked on his door without success earlier. She went inside. I heard a muffled conversation in the front room. She returned. "He doesn't want to speak to you."

The only direct contact began one Saturday morning, with a message on my phone at 7.48am.

"I'll call you back later 'cos I'm not at home and I'm on a mobile," he said. After a few seconds pause, he added, almost as an afterthought: "My name's Dawson," followed by a mumbled but distinctly audible, "You bastard".

His voice was firm and clear when we spoke an hour later, but his boasts from years before had evaporated: "I don't know anything about it. All I know is that Kelso Cochrane was murdered. I was in prison at the time. Don't believe what you read in *The People*." His belief in his former leader nevertheless remained undimmed. "Oswald Mosley was a great patriot and a great man."

CHAPTER FOUR

MORE NEWS FROM NOWHERE

*"It is easy, as Lucretius observed, to stand on the shore
and pass judgement on the work of those battling against
the wind and waves in a high sea."*
Appeal Court judgement, Regina v Ram, 1995.

The parallels are striking. Around five white youths launch an unprovoked attack on an innocent black man on a London street at night. One of them drives a knife deep into him. There are witnesses, but none can identify the assailants accurately enough to sustain a conviction. The murder occurs in an area targeted by the far-right, and which is home to a tightly-knit community with a large criminal population who look dimly on those who assist the police. The perpetrators' names are whispered around the neighbourhood. At the outset police deny a racial motive in the crime. The killers evade justice.

The similarities between the murder of 18-year-old Stephen Lawrence near a bus stop in Eltham, south east London in April 1993, and that of Kelso Cochrane in Notting Hill forty-four years before are overwhelming. Both became cause célèbres which activists united around, demanding change. Both attracted much publicity: Kelso's an initial rush before the case faded sharply from view, Stephen Lawrence's a little at first, then enough to burn itself irrevocably into the public consciousness. Both were watersheds in the history of British race relations. Kelso's put anti-racism on the national agenda, galvanising the crusade for laws against discrimination. The first Race Relations Act was finally passed in 1965, six years after he was killed. Stephen Lawrence's death did nothing less than change the terms of the debate on race in Britain.

But the resonances between the cases shouldn't obscure the differences. There are the contrasting social and political climates for a start. In 1959 the authorities viewed Notting Hill - with its overcrowding, thousands of newly arrived West Indian immigrants and recent major racial conflagration - as a powder keg. The random killing of a black man in the district brimmed with wider dangers, sending tremors from Whitehall to the Caribbean. Eltham in 1993 hardly generated such fears.

Then there are the fates of those who committed the crimes. While the young men widely held to be responsible for killing Stephen Lawrence have been outed and written about for years, those involved in Kelso's murder disappeared into the shadows, free to settle into lives of quiet respectability and obscurity, perhaps surrounded by children and grandchildren with no idea of their dark secret. But what of the conviction, especially among black people, that in both instances the killers escaped justice because of police racism?

Hundreds of hours of testimony at the public inquiry into Stephen Lawrence's murder led Sir William Macpherson to famously conclude that the Metropolitan police were "institutionally racist" and that "fundamental errors" littered their investigation, especially in its early stages.

Meanwhile, for those who lived through the era when shoving black suspects' heads down a toilet bowl and flushing the chain was, it's claimed, a favoured interrogation technique of some police officers, the belief that Kelso's life was considered to be worth less than his killer's remains unshakeable. An ageing Ladbroke Grove hustler, all too familiar with the inside of Harrow Road station, almost spits the words out: "To them he was just a broken bottle. A black broken bottle lying on the street." The police, naturally, strongly contest this.

* * *

Stanley Cochrane received an initial acknowledgment to his letter asking for his brother's murder to be re-investigated, which he wrote after waking from a troubled sleep one night in March 2003. Six months later, another letter arrived. The police had now completed their enquiries and "regrettably there was insufficient evidence for any realistic prospect of a conviction". Stanley wasn't leaving it at that. He decided to come to England to see if he could somehow drive things forward before it was too late, arriving in London for only the second time in his life in November 2004.

Barry Howe, a highly experienced former Detective Chief Inspector had led the "focussed forensic review" into Kelso's case. Howe had come out of retirement to work for the Met's Serious Crime Review Group. His job was to find new clues in a backlog of old murders. Sifting through the voluminous Kelso Cochrane files - which not unusually in such cases, remain closed to the public because of legal sensitivities until January 2044 - Howe saw that significant resources and man-hours had been devoted to the original investigation, with almost 1,000 statements taken.

Some honour would have been attached to finally getting a conviction in such a symbolic case after all these years. Success might even have helped repair the Met's reputation in the wake of Macpherson. Yet when Stanley met him, Barry Howe told him that there simply wasn't the evidence to charge anyone. Advances in forensic science were no use, as no forensic opportunities existed: there was no murder weapon to test for DNA, no clothes to test for fibres or blood. Kelso's had been destroyed in 1968 "with the proper authority".

What about witnesses? Surely now, with any lingering threat to their safety receding, someone with direct knowledge of the murder might come forward and testify? At a distance of almost half a century, the quality of their evidence would have to be remarkably robust. Any half-competent defence lawyer would dismantle the story of someone who'd waited decades to speak - particularly if they'd given a statement in 1959 they now retracted.

A young woman detective was assigned to answer Stanley's questions and offer support. She tried her best to reassure him, saying that a surprising number of cases like his brother's were solved with deathbed confessions. Stanley wasn't convinced.

"They [the police] said if it happened now with CCTV they would have solved it within two or three days," he said later. "The long and short of it was that no one was able to identify the person who committed the murder and they have no forensic evidence. I suggested to them look at the cases of Ku Klux Klan in America, and how they're [still] getting results. There's no resolution in this matter. The police claim they don't have enough evidence. So go and get the evidence. We want a satisfactory resolution to the demise of my brother."

* * *

November 2005. Howe's impression of the exhaustive nature of Forbes-Leith's inquiry was echoed by one of the officers on it.

A tall, upright man in his early eighties with a bluff, no-nonsense manner - a legacy, perhaps, of 25 years in the CID and a war served in the RAF - he appeared weary and a little distracted. He didn't want his name in print, but was willing to share his recollections with me.

He was only a junior detective at the time, so the key decisions were above him: his main roles were supervising the search for the knife in the local drains and the Grand Union Canal, and conducting door-to-door enquiries.

Working in X Division, the Met operational district in which the murder occurred, was intense. "It was an area with a strange mix. A lot of villains. Everyone would get pissed at the weekends and it wasn't uncommon to have to deal with four or five GBHs in a night...We came across some amazing sights during the investigation. I remember walking down the road and seeing a bride and groom who'd just got married perched on the back of a coal lorry."

Policing was very different then, before the days of mission statements and best-value performance indicators. "At Harrow Road we only had one van, so most of our patrols were on foot. There were no walkie-talkies. Every statement was duplicated or triplicated by the station's typist. You could work 18 hours in a day with no overtime and weren't well-paid." But the powers were far greater. There was no Police and Criminal Evidence Act, with its codes of practice for interviewing and detaining suspects. No Crown Prosecution Service to decide whether or not to prosecute. "You could nick someone in the morning, have them up in the magistrate's court by lunchtime and sentenced and in prison by the afternoon," he explained. Suspects could be held for up to three days without being charged and without access to a lawyer. It was, in his view, "so much more efficient than now."

As to the murder: "It was all over in seconds and if you'd been there you may not have even seen it. There were witnesses. But no-one actually saw the knife go in."

He had little doubt who'd done it. There just wasn't enough to peg it on.

Maybe, he conceded, Ian Forbes-Leith's upper-crust background played some part in the outcome. "He was completely out of place among the villains of the Dale," he said. 'The governor in the bowler', as he was known, wouldn't countenance the more heavy-handed tactics another boss might have deployed in the same circumstances. Hamstrung by a lack of witnesses, but with a good idea of the perpetrator, it wasn't unknown for the police to play suspects off against each other until one of them 'rolled over', or to make the lives of the local villainy so unbearable that they finally gave up the guilty party.

Straying into far more dubious territory, was the use of 'verbals': false claims that a suspect had made a verbal confession. "Nice bloke" that Forbes-Leith was, said his old colleague, this just wasn't his way.

The old detective seemed genuinely upset. "It was a shame," he said, ushering me to his front door. "Kelso came across as a hardworking man in interviews with the people who knew him. It broke our hearts not being able to get anyone."

* * *

On the face of it then, the failure to charge anyone for the murder ultimately lies in that conundrum of modern policing: the gap between believing something to be true, and being able to prove it. In being able to build a case on hard facts, rather than hearsay. In having forensic evidence - albeit of the basic kind available in 1959, of matching fingerprints, blood groups or clothes fibres - and having none. Between, on the one hand, being able to place someone in the vicinity of the murder at the relevant time, and on the other, having credible witnesses prepared to stand up and testify in court - withstanding rigorous cross-examination by defence counsel and likely intimidation by the suspects' associates - exactly who did what when, in an event which happened in the dark and was over in an instant.

This explanation for why Kelso's killer has remained free - along with his accomplices, who might have been charged with conspiracy to murder before or after the fact - has credibility and supporting evidence. Yet it's by no means the whole story. Documents that remained classified for forty-five years begin to shed a less favourable light on the Kelso Cochrane investigation.

* * *

Detective Superintendent Ian Forbes-Leith. "The Governor in
the Bowler."
Copyright: Solo Syndication.

Wednesday May 20, 1959. Breakfast time at Harrow Road. Some
80 hours earlier and half a mile away, Kelso lay dying on the
street. A young police constable called Colin Wilson was in the

canteen when he was handed a brown envelope, addressed to *John Wilson Esq, 325 Harrow Road, W9*. PC Wilson was the only officer at the station with that surname. He opened it.

May 19, 1959

Dear Mr Wilson,
Many thanks for your excellent information regarding the Notting Hill murder early on Sunday morning. This is the type of hot news that we always seek and I shall be glad to have an opportunity of meeting you.
If you could ring me on the News Desk extension 268 we can arrange a meeting.
Look forward to meeting you.

Edward Gartell, Deputy News Editor

Wilson thought it was a joke, and a pretty sick one: someone had probably tipped off the paper and used his name. He showed the letter to his colleagues, and then burnt it.

The following Saturday a second letter arrived at Harrow Road for John Wilson with the same stamp across the top right of the envelope as the first: '*Daily Express - Britain's Liveliest Newspaper*'. Inside was a cheque for £10 and an invoice that said: '*Description of contribution: Harrow Road murder tip exc. £10.*'

Realising it wasn't a prank PC Wilson informed Det Supt Forbes-Leith, who told his immediate superiors, who in turn notified Scotland Yard's top brass. An exchange of memos followed between Commander George Hatherill, head of CID, whom Forbes-Leith had reported to in the lengthy Brighton police corruption case, Met Commissioner Sir Joseph Simpson, a Trenchard man like Forbes-Leith, and Sir Theobald Matthew, the long-serving Director of Public Prosecutions. Something, they decided, must be done. A newspaper paying the police for stories, even if it was £10, was illegal. Moreover, leaking the details of a murder soon after it had occurred - before the victim's next-of-kin had even been informed - could potentially hamper an investigation.

The story in question had hit the streets at 4am. *"A coloured man was stabbed to death in a street brawl in Notting Hill early today,"* it read under the headline, *Murder in Notting Hill. "Three youths were believed to have been involved in the fight. Detective Superintendent Ian Forbes-Leith, ex-Scotland Yard murder squad detective, who took over the Division CID only a few weeks ago was called from his bed to take charge of the investigation. He arrived in Golborne Road, Notting Hill within an hour of the murder..."*

The *Sunday Express* had somehow obtained facts known only to a very few at that time, had the story lino-typed, set and copied on to a metal cylinder, which was put into heavy machinery. The newspaper was printed and on sale just over three hours after Kelso's death.

There was nothing unusual in this: tips flowed constantly from the police to the press. In fact, there had been three internal inquiries in the previous three years into leaks from X Division alone. In each case the press had arrived at the scene of a major crime as swiftly as the emergency services, and before the news had been released. In none of the inquiries was the source uncovered, and the idea was floated, though not with any real conviction, that journalists might be using short wave wireless receivers to tune into the police's wavelengths. With Kelso Cochrane this was impossible, as no wireless messages had been sent.

Two senior officers, Detective Superintendent Lewis and Detective Chief Inspector Mackay were ordered to find the culprit. In the intensity of a major murder inquiry, the unwelcome sub-plot of an internal disciplinary investigation had begun.

They started whittling down those who knew the vital facts at the given time, and had the means to leak them.

What about Ken Steele, Horatio Lewis and George Isaacs, the three Samaritans who rushed to Kelso's aid that night, taking him to St Charles' Hospital? Impossible. They were under police supervision at the critical time. And PC Wilson, who opened the two letters? He was in bed at 11 o'clock after finishing a shift that Saturday. It was soon obvious that no uniformed officer from Harrow Road was responsible; that the information in the *Sunday Express* could only have come from a CID man very close to the inquiry in its early stages.

Lewis and Mackay met the paper's editor John Junor at his Fleet Street office, and told him that they were there on the instructions of the Director of Public Prosecutions and that if they didn't discover the informant's identity "some innocent, unfortunate" officer might be blamed. Junor promised his full cooperation, and claimed that the *Sunday Express* would never knowingly send money to a policeman. The officers moved on to the journalists responsible for the story: Frank Draper and John Ponder.

Draper, a junior reporter, claimed he'd received the initial tip-off. The more he spoke, the less convincing he was.

"It was between two and three in the morning, nearer three I should say, when a man phoned up and said he wanted to tell us about a murder at Golborne Road, Notting Hill," he told the officers. "I asked him for his name and address first and he was reluctant to give it. He said three white youths had stabbed a darkie named Cochrane, but I should say the name Cochrane is known to me now, and it may be that he gave a name that sounded like Cochrane and could have been Corkrane."

The reporter's recollections of the odd caller and their bizarre conversation seemed to change with every telling. The man's voice "was rough and somewhat hesitant", he said. Or he sounded like "a drunken Irishman". In fact, now Draper came to think of it, the mystery informant sounded like Johnny 'Scarface'

Carter, a sharp-dressed East End crook who hung around Bayswater, and was well-known for feeding newspapers juicy stories. According to criminal folklore, Carter had once entered a pub followed by a friend with a double-barrel shotgun; his friend pumped several shots into the pub's ceiling and ran off; Carter phoned a newspaper to sell a dramatic eyewitness account of the event.

Frank Draper was flannelling. That Johnny Carter or an intoxicated Irishman knew the details of the murder at that time, the victim's name and that Ian Forbes-Leith was leading the inquiry, was barely plausible. It made even less sense considering the *Sunday Express* had sent a cheque for the story to Harrow Road police station. Lewis told Draper he didn't believe him. In their notes, the officers described Draper as "the sort of man who would tell any story if it suited his purpose". John Ponder, who they turned to next, was damned as "very silly" and "the most indiscreet man in Fleet Street".

"You got an exclusive story very early, didn't you?" Lewis began.

"Yes, we did, didn't we," Ponder agreed.

"How did you get it?"

"Someone rang up and I made the rest up myself. I knew who would be on the inquiry."

Ponder then offered various explanations for how he stood the story up.

"Verification from Back Hall [Scotland Yard] old chap."

"Nonsense," said Lewis.

"Well, it was actually someone at St Charles' Hospital."

"They didn't know."

"It was a uniformed officer who rang up, but he gave another policemen's name to get him into trouble."

"That's quite wrong. No uniformed officer knew that youths were involved," said Lewis. "Only CID officers investigating the murder knew that."

"I can assure you Mr Forbes-Leith is not the person." Ponder had known him since the Brighton corruption case.

"How can you say Mr Forbes-Leith is not concerned when you yourself say you don't know who phoned?"

"You're wrong if you think it's Mr Forbes-Leith."

It was clear where this was leading.

"I am not paid to think anything. The facts may speak up for themselves."

"Oh dear, can't we square this up somehow?" suggested Ponder. "I don't want to be put up against the police. I wish this had never happened."

Lewis raised Ponder's approach, a few hours after the murder, to Detective Sergeant John Merry, the police photographer who'd raised himself from his bed in Croydon and headed over to west London to photograph the crime scene. At 4.45am Merry had dropped in at Scotland Yard to pick up his equipment on his way to Harrow Road. Ponder spotted him at the entrance and handed him a copy of that day's paper with news of the killing on the front page.

"You remember me John," he'd said. "My name's John Ponder from the *Sunday Express*. Are you going to Harrow Road? John, would you do me a favour and give this copy personally to Mr Forbes-Leith... Now don't forget my name. It's most important. John Ponder."

"That was a little pointed wasn't it?" said Lewis.

"No, not at all. I don't agree. It was just my way of trying to impress the Detective Superintendent, rather than upset him by letting him see that I had given him some publicity, and if you like, hoping that perhaps later on people wouldn't turn their backs on me when I tried to get some more information."

"Look," Lewis said finally, "it's no good you trying to protect your informant - the facts speak up for themselves."

"I am sorry this has happened. I've always tried to be best of friends with the police. I would be very upset indeed if things go wrong over this," Ponder said, though he still resisted naming his source.

By now, Mackay and Lewis had concluded that only three CID officers could have been responsible for the leak.

Sid Coomber: the silver-haired, 42-year-old Detective Sergeant who arrived at St Charles' shortly after Kelso, and who had assisted hospital staff as they frantically tried to keep him alive. Eighteen years before, Coomber had been awarded the George Medal for rescuing several seriously injured men from a building that was collapsing after being bombed by the Luftwaffe.

Ferguson Walker: a lugubrious Detective Inspector with a droopy moustache, Walker had worked for twenty-one hours straight and only got a couple of hours rest before Coomber called his home in Wembley and he dragged himself back to Harrow Road.

And Ian Forbes-Leith: as an ex-senior investigator for the Yard's murder squad, he was among the exclusive band of officers entitled to wear the unit's signature maroon tie decorated with a globe and dagger. Just two years before he had been lauded as 'The pride of Hendon College' for uncovering the corruption festering in Brighton Borough Police.

Thursday July 16, 1959. Sir Joseph Simpson summoned the three men. He was quite satisfied one or more had leaked the story, he said, and unless he found out who, *"they would not go any further"* - meaning their chances of promotion were over.

Thursday August 6, 1959. The leak inquiry was taking its toll. "This matter is causing great distress to us and our families," wrote Forbes-Leith in a memo to his superiors proclaiming his innocence. He maintained that neither he, Walker nor Coomber had the motive nor the opportunity to pass on the information; that they all knew that around six youths had attacked Kelso - not three, as the *Sunday Express* article stated; and that the most likely suspects were the officers on duty in the area wireless car.

"I am satisfied that I and my two colleagues will be exonerated and the true suspects indicated," he wrote.

Wednesday November 11, 1959. For six months it had drawn on, but finally the inquiry was finally over. No further action was to be taken. Forbes-Leith, despite his declarations of innocence, was not exonerated. Lewis and Mackay's report landed on Sir Joseph Simpson's desk. *"John Wilson"*, it stated, was a nom de plume and *"the extraordinarily clumsy cheque payment was an error...It was never intended by the two reporters concerned to be sent to a police officer, but that one of them was to endorse and cash it (whether or not the police officer got any of it, in any form, subsequently)."*

As to the source of the leak, Lewis wrote: *"I have spent some time with Detective Inspector Walker and Detective Sergeant Coomber and as a result of many questions I have discovered nothing which suggests either of them is responsible for the leakage of information which was so vital to the inquiry. Mr Forbes-Leith has made a statement in which he reports he did not have any contact with the representatives of any newspaper."*

Everything pointed towards the source being the man leading the murder hunt. Upon being woken at home at 1.15 in the morning with news of the stabbing, Ian Forbes-Leith had probably, almost as a reflex, picked up the phone and called his old contact John Ponder to tip him off. Consequently, in the midst of a highly-charged murder inquiry with serious public order implications, his career - as well as Fergie Walker's and Sid Coomber's - was under threat, and they had to spend many hours defending their reputations. Could this possibly have had any effect on the investigation's failure? Who, all these years later, could say?

Not the old detective I'd met.

Not Sid Coomber, who had died in Oxfordshire in 2005 at the age of 89.

And not Ian Forbes-Leith, whose police career never did *"go any further"* after Kelso Cochrane. He investigated other big cases - the death of Jean Johnson, a young St Lucian mother found stabbed in a basement flat in Paddington in November 1959, and that of 78-year-old Fred Skinner, discovered strangled in a garden in Harlesden on Christmas morning 1960 - but his rapid climb through the Met ranks was over. On 27 February 1961, a small item headed *Police Chief to Resign* appeared at the bottom of the *Daily Telegraph* front page:

"Det Supt Ian Forbes-Leith, 44, who was the youngest officer ever appointed by Scotland Yard to this senior rank, is to resign from the Metropolitan Police. He will leave the force on March 24 to take up a commercial appointment. He is leaving after 25 years service. It is more usual for officers to complete 30 years to obtain a higher pension rate. Only 38 when promoted to Detective Superintendent, during the last six years he has served in London's East and West Ends. He was appointed two years ago to X Division and soon quelled the rising crime wave in the Harrow Road area..."

He ended up in a quiet little Berkshire hamlet and had died years ago.

While Forbes-Leith's police career stalled in 1959, and finished abruptly 18 months later, Ferguson Walker's thrived. By 1967 he was a superintendent, and known for a deep knowledge of the underworld from Soho to the East End. He was so highly thought of that he was handed one of the Yard's most sensitive tasks - ending the Kray twins bloody reign in London - but after a few largely fruitless months, Walker was promoted to Chief Superintendent and transferred to another department, and the case was passed on.

In the view of an old colleague, Fergie may have drunk less than his contemporaries, but he was still: "typical old-school CID, but a bit cannier and lower-key than most." As Forbes-Leith's number two, he'd surely have known the inner-workings of the Kelso investigation, and what other secrets, if any, it might have held.

* * *

July 2009. It felt like somewhere an old detective would retire: a tranquil corner of Surrey with big houses with long gravel drives, a commuter hinterland dotted with golf courses, tennis courts and tree-shaded avenues. Fergie's house was tucked away at the end of a little close, and was more modest than those on the walk from the station. The place looked dark and uninhabited, and a pile of mail lay on the doormat inside. His neighbour proved helpful. Fergie, he said, was at a nursing home a couple of miles away. He'd had two hip replacements, but was apparently still mentally sharp.

"I'm sure Jock would love to speak to you about the old days," said the friendly nurse when I arrived at the care home, which looked more like a stately country residence. "But I'll have to call his daughter first to clear it." She led me into an office full of files, dug out the details, called the number and handed me the phone. The woman on the other end was brusque.

Absolutely not...He's almost 90...How did you find him?

And no, she wouldn't meet me so that I could try to reassure her and explain more.

The door was slammed shut and a follow-up letter failed to prise it open. The last breathing witness to the upper reaches of the investigation would be keeping whatever he knew within the care home's walls.

* * *

May 1976. John Ponder: postscript. Fifteen years after the £10 cheque debacle, John Ponder faced far more serious pressure for his contacts with the police. By then he was the chief crime correspondent of the *Evening Standard*, and was charged with dishonestly handling police photos and inducing an officer to commit a breach of discipline, after he'd received pictures from a police source of three men charged with a murder. Ponder refused to name his source, and as his trial approached sank into depression and shot himself in the thigh. He survived - but his spleen was wrecked and his career ruined. After he was finally cleared of the charges, he made a statement on the symbiotic relationship between the press and the police and the widespread practice of officers passing stories to select journalists: "I believe I was a scapegoat and I was used to stop the long-accepted system of individual police officers and journalists sharing confidential relationships," he said.

CHAPTER FIVE

PAST MEETS PRESENT

December 2005 – December 2010

"The past recedes, lapping back from a muddied shore across which it's unsafe to wade." Will Self.

His front door had extra locks, and on my first few visits there was no answer. When he finally let me in, Shoggy Breagan said he'd been there all the time, peering through the spy-hole. "You've gotta watch yourself," he explained in a rasping voice. "You can't even be safe in your own home."

Shoggy lived alone on his state pension in a little council flat in a cul-de-sac near the A40 motorway. He had the height and frame of an old jockey, and the shoulders of an ex-middleweight boxer. His dark hair was thinning and most of his bottom teeth were gone. It was early afternoon but he was in his dressing gown and slippers.

He was friendly, and apologised for the state of the place. "D'you mind if I have a cigarette?" he asked, despite being in his own kitchen. Pictures from the *Sun* of Freddie Flintoff celebrating England's Ashes' triumph and of Frank Lampard controlling a football were pinned on one wall. Another had a small dent - from an incident he later hazily recounted involving an old neighbour.

He moved away from the table, where a mobile phone and a packet of Golden Virginia lay by a Chelsea FC mug, its inside rimmed with tea stains, opened the window on the other side of the room and stood blowing the smoke outside.

"When I go, I hope I've done something good in this world,"

he said. "I've kept my kids out of prison. The one thing I've done is keep my sons out of prison." A life of crime was fading into one of loneliness and regret, and he seemed to be clinging to this thought like a life-raft.

His path towards some lengthy stretches in jail had begun in another era. In April 1949, when he was 15 and the second oldest of eight kids growing up in Wilsham Street, Notting Dale, he'd been caught "shop-breaking with intent" and fined 2/6d at Stamford Juvenile Court. Six months later, Shoggy - the name came from his uncle, a local totter - was arrested for "stealing a bicycle pedal" and given 12 months probation. In February 1953, he received his first custodial sentence, for "stealing property worth £60 in a dwelling house", and was sent for borstal training. In between, there were stints of work: as an apprentice French Polisher for Liddell and King Ltd on Norland Road, W11 (his character was described as "good"), as a van boy for Walters Palm Toffee Limited in East Acton (there too, his character was described as "good"), and as a labourer at Kelly Builders in Camberwell. But his criminal résumé got progressively worse, and soon dwarfed his employment record.

A retired policeman who arrested him in 1960 after he'd failed to show at court for attempting to steal from a car, remembered him without a pause. The officer turned up at the property where Shoggy was holed-up in Colville Terrace, which was owned by the notorious slum landlord Peter Rachman, and a tussle ensued as he tried to escape. "He was one of the local pond-life," the officer recalled, "the failed children who didn't have much of a chance who were all thrown in together, fell into the hands of the police and Juvenile Courts at a young age and lived by the law of the jungle."

By the time he was thirty-seven, his probation officer, Miss CJ Garbet, described him as a "recidivist" who impressed her as "easily led". "He was very co-operative in interviews talking readily about himself," she wrote, adding: "He admits to spending a lot of his time in clubs where he does a lot of social drinking."

* * *

Shoggy disappeared into the back bedroom, where a blue-and-white Chelsea flag was draped across the window, then returned to the kitchen with remnants from his past: a black-and-white photo of him in his twenties lying contentedly on the grass with a young woman on a warm day; a portrait of generations of his family; another of him surrounded by smiling workmates outside a big house in Kensington where he worked as a labourer in the 1980s - the house belonged to one of the rock group Queen, he said. Finally, there was the eulogy from his mother Edith's funeral in 1994.

The memories tumbled out. "Great days. I had a good life, a good mother. I loved my mum. She was a lady. She used to visit me in prison and people used to ask if she was my sister...We all think we're Jack the lad when we're young. Untouchable. I was out night and day. I used to knock around Powis Terrace. I used to knock around with a lot of blacks. I knew a lot of prostitutes. They were diamonds."

"Back then the old Bill were characters. You knew where you stood with coppers then. When you're up to no good the police always got their uppers. I'm not saying they picked on me, 'cos the old saying in those days was 'the police knew'. They would 'verbal' you up, but you took it..."

But his tearaway days were ancient history. He didn't get out much now, and when he did, he enjoyed going to cemeteries and museums. "I've been to more funerals than Hugh Grant... My ex-wife was down here. I moan and groan, but never about prison."

* * *

Of the scores of young men who traipsed through Harrow Road police station in the wake of Kelso Cochrane's murder, Shoggy Breagan and Patrick Digby were detained the longest, for around 50 hours each, before the police escorted them to their homes 150 yards apart in the Dale, where they were greeted by well-wishers.

Shoggy was sitting at his kitchen table when I explained why I'd appeared from nowhere on his doorstep. It was probably years, maybe decades, since anyone had asked him about Kelso Cochrane. The moment I did, he seemed to freeze, and his eyes, which were startlingly clear, began to well-up. It felt like he was on the brink: perhaps something fateful, something with far-reaching consequences that he'd been carrying inside for years, was about to be unburdened?

But just when it seemed his emotions might overwhelm him, he regained composure and began his account - sometimes clear, occasionally befuddled - of what happened fifty years before. Over the next twelve months he added fragments to it in rambling calls at odd hours, some of them from phone boxes.

The recollections of Shoggy Breagan:

"It was Bank Holiday 1959. I came out of Maidstone Prison after serving three years and I went to a party on Southam Street. I took Pat Digby to the party and there was something said between us, so I asked him outside for a fight. Nothing came of it so we went back to the party. Me and Patsy got on okay. We had a row going on. But we were nowhere near there [where Kelso was stabbed]. How I ever got home that night I don't know."

"I came out of my house on the Sunday. I walked in to the Warwick Arms at dinner time and they told me a black bloke's been stabbed. I was drinking all day." Just before midnight he got back to Wilsham Street. "When I got home the door was open and the police were waiting for me. They shouted out to me, 'Shoggy we want you.' I bolted the door. They come in and said we want to see you for questioning. My mum said, 'Last time you questioned him, he got three years.'" Shoggy ran out of the back. "I wandered round and didn't know where to go. I walked round for half an hour." The police took his mother in a squad car to search the streets for him, but eventually he said, he went to Harrow Road of his own accord.

There a detective made a comment that had stuck with him. "He said to me, 'You've got a bit of spink in you.' I said, 'What's that?' He said, 'A bit of black in you.'" Shoggy was tanned from hours spent on the football pitch at Maidstone prison.

Forensic tests were carried out. "They took samples of my blood and everything. My clothes were examined. The suit I had on was the same suit I had on Saturday night."

Pat Digby had already been questioned by the time the police interviewed Shoggy for the first time. The young men's accounts of the night basically tallied - except in one respect: their explanations for leaving Ma O'Brien's party. "Patsy had told them we were going to have a fight. I never said that." Breagan said they'd left the party to look for girls. He was taken to the cells.

Shoggy was left to sweat it out through Tuesday and most of Wednesday while the police tried to corroborate their stories, and after being interviewed again, was told he could go.

"They took me home. All the newspapers and the cameras were there. The next day the paper said I went to the cinema but I didn't." He said the police had never been in touch about it again and that the last time he'd seen Patsy was about ten years ago getting on a train at Ealing Broadway. "We were best of pals."

He insisted, time and again, that he was innocent. "I never done it." And he didn't know who did. "I don't know. I don't know till this day. The police never mentioned any names to me."

I told him that Stanley Cochrane was still tormented by thoughts of his brother's death, and still searching for the truth.

"I do feel really sorry for the brother. I can understand. I've got sons myself. They said Kelso Cochrane was a nice, quiet fella. As far as I know this man was a decent, honest, working-class man."

In one of the calls that followed, this time out of the blue at 7am one summer morning, he claimed that he'd become emotional when we'd met because he'd been thinking about his mum, and veered from one thought to the next:

"Prison sends you loopy...We're not all saints in Notting Hill...If you want to see what Southam Street looked like in those days, watch *Sapphire*." Shot partly in Notting Hill in the aftermath of the riots, the film was about the murder of a mixed-race girl found dead on Hampstead Heath.

After that, I heard nothing from Shoggy for years, despite my periodic efforts to contact him. Then one day a familiar voice called on an unfamiliar number.

"You know I had a stroke. They said I had - what is it, I forget now? Sugar diabetes. I was walking down the road and the next morning I went to get out of bed I fell on the floor. The next thing there was a knock at the door. It was my two boys on their dinner break come down to see dad. They was shouting 'Dad, dad, you alright?' I said 'No, I can't move'. I was crawling on the floor. They went downstairs and got a stick and put their hands through the letter-box and opened it. They took me straight to hospital. I can't hardly walk now. I miss my walking mate."

He'd just lost a sister and a nephew, and was going to the latter's funeral at Kensal Green Cemetery in two days. "I ain't slept a lot since my sister and nephew died, cos' he was a gentleman my nephew. I'm a lucky, lucky man. I've got the best family in Notting Hill. If it hadn't been for my family - well, I would never have killed myself, I haven't got the guts to kill myself - but I would've have been lost. There are some arsehole friends, but one good pal comes to see me three or four times a month. I've been nicked with the man four times...I had a good time in prison in the 60s and 70s when prisons was prisons. We done it the hard way, but we done it well. I've had better Christmases in prison than I've had out here. "

"... I've got a black sister-in-law, black nieces and nephews. I know more black people than you'll ever know in your life. Diamonds, a lot of black people, diamonds. They all know Shoggy. We might have had our rows but they were good people in the 50s. They know I'm innocent."

And that was it.

* * *

So why Shoggy Breagan? What drew the police so rapidly to his door? On the night of the killing, there were any number of young men in the locality whose past form would have attracted their interest; a few had been arrested during the riots eight months before. But being incarcerated at the time, Shoggy wasn't one of them.

The crime for which he was in jail, had been committed with two other men, and was described by prosecuting counsel at the Old Bailey as: *"a vicious, yet entirely unprovoked attack with knives on three coloured men who were peacefully walking towards their homes late at night in the Paddington district of London."*

Sentencing them to three years for grievous bodily harm, Judge Aarvold said: *"It is quite dreadful to think that anybody in this country could behave in such a way you three behaved on this night. Apparently you have been misled into some sort of colour prejudice or colour hatred. You allowed yourselves to become affected by drink to such an extent that you behaved like hooligans and almost ran amok among such coloured people as you could find, and you used against them weapons, including a knife."*

On Thursday May 7, 1959 - nine days before Kelso's murder - Breagan was released from prison. Yet a defendant's previous convictions aren't put before a jury for the good reason that they should be judged solely on the strength of the evidence against them. Shoggy's antecedents, likewise, don't mean he's guilty. In fact, it's safe to go much further: whatever he knew, however bad his record, and despite his emotional reaction at the first mention of the dead man's name, Shoggy Breagan did not kill Kelso Cochrane.

* * *

Wild West Eleven

Pictures of generations of his family in carefully posed group shots hung across his living room wall. Beside him was an oxygen cylinder attached to a mask, which he grasped to his mouth at regular intervals, sucking in air to stay alive.

Peter Bell pointed the remote control at the television, turned down the volume, and looked over at me. Gold-rimmed spectacles framed his blue eyes and his dark hair had a touch of grey. He wore a spotless white vest, grey tracksuit bottoms and blue slippers. "Love" and "Hate" were tattooed across his knuckles in fading blue ink. "I got to 69. I ain't done bad," he began. "I've been shot. I've been stabbed. They said I wouldn't get to 21 'cos I was a nutty bastard, thought I would've been dead long ago."

But he was living in a state of advanced physical collapse, his life barely extending beyond the couch where he spent his waking hours watching TV. He had gout and the beginnings of Parkinson's. He wore a pacemaker, and for the past 12 years he'd had emphysema. Staggering up the short flight of stairs to the bedroom above took half an hour, he said. He could only walk six steps continuously, and apparently hadn't been out of the house for a year. Still, there was no way he was having a stair lift fitted: "It'd ruin the house".

At night he slept upright - if he slumped, his airways contracted and he awoke frantically gasping for breath. "Like someone's putting a pillow over your mouth." His doctor said he'd soon have to be hooked-up to the oxygen machine for 15 hours a day, but he was resigned to it: "Fuck it. We're all going to die."

With trembling hands, he lit one cigarette after another. He couldn't roll them himself because of the Parkinson's. "I've been smoking since I was 10. It's killing me, but I can't fucking stop. At night I think I'll give up, but in the day I always have one. I told the doctor I've given up, and every time I see him he says he can see the improvement." The booze was different. No one believed he'd do it, but he hadn't had a drink for almost 40 years. "I was near-enough alcoholic. I was on the wine in the mornings, drinking seven days a week. Fuck that. It made me go potty. If I'd carried on someone would have killed me, or I'd have killed someone."

I handed him a copy of the *Daily Express* article which appeared four days after Kelso was stabbed; the story which was headlined *The posse in tight trousers hunts a killer,* and which told how a group of local young men had set out to help solve the crime:

"...They had all been questioned by police at Harrow Road police station. And 12 of their friends joined them to find out who stabbed 32-year-old West Indian Kelso Cochrane on Whit Sunday. The young men - in tight trousers, pointed shoes and slicked down hair - began to comb out the score of clubs in the streets of crumbling houses within half a mile of the murder corner on Southam Street. They went around in little groups and conducted the search in whispers over glasses of beer in the dingy club rooms where juke boxes played harshly, lights burned softly and girls in flared skirts jived. One of the self-appointed 'Notting Hill Squad' 22-year-old Peter Bell of Talbot Grove, said: 'We are not doing this for the sake of the police. Two of our mates are still at the police station. The police say this could be a hanging job and we don't want any suspicion attached to any of us.'...He said: 'We may not be angels round here, but we don't stand for knifing. So we are going to put

ourselves around and make it our business to dig this one out.'"

"Fucking hell. Is that me?" Peter said, squinting at his picture from almost fifty years before, and then putting the cutting to one side.

We began to work our way back. Chatting about two things, at least, seemed to lift his spirits: the past and Notting Hill. "It was better in them days," he said. "The world we're living in now is fucking sadistic. It's horrible. Cunts out for themselves."

* * *

The Bells' infamy had long faded, but once, with their friends the Bakers, they were among Notting Dale's most notorious families. It was a reputation that briefly soared beyond the confines of W10 and W11 in 1960, when Peter, his dad Big Ernie, older brother Ernie junior and younger one Sydney, along with 'Little' Georgie Baker, stood trial at the Old Bailey. It wasn't every day, after all, that a father, three sons and their mate were all charged with the same murder.

There were seven Bell children in total, and even more Bakers, with Georgie the eldest of eight. One story, repeated so often it's assumed the status of a copper-bottomed fact, goes that old man Baker, who stood all of 5ft 2in, once cleared the Ladbroke pub by eating a live mouse between two slices of bread. The other drinkers retched as he spat the innards into his beer glass.

The Bells and Bakers lived a few doors apart on Talbot Grove, just off Ladbroke Grove; the Bells at numbers 11 and 14, the Bakers at 13. For a while, the street's defining feature was the open rubbish dump on a waste plot where it met St Mark's Road. Indignation about this "blot on the 20th century standards of hygiene and public health" simmered in the *Kensington News* for more than a year. In August 1957 the paper described it as containing "every conceivable item of rubbish, half-burnt mattresses, rusted springs, broken bottles and a dead pigeon with scores of blue-flies hovering around."

A year later it was even worse. "This site is 3ft high with rotting, decaying vegetable matter and unrecognisable animal matter. On a cold day the stench is clearly distinguishable. On a hot day when all the young children of Talbot Grove want to be out playing, the smell is abominable. Until quite recently there were dead cats and chickens on the dump. Sometimes maggots can be seen crawling on the rubbish. Fires are a frequent occurrence on the site. Youngsters have set fire to mattresses left there by rag and bone men who can find no market for them. There are scorch marks 30ft high up one side." It was, in short: "480 square feet of public disgrace."

Residents petitioned the Council. "I have been trying for over three years to get something done," GC Dyett complained to the *Kensington News*. "The only thing I can get from the Council is that the owner of the land cannot be found. Is this then all the Council intend doing - nothing? - because some unfortunate man or woman cannot or will not pay for a worthless piece of ground and are content to just forget that they owned it."

* * *

Peter Bell was enjoying talking about the old days. He drew on another roll-up. If he didn't have a fag in his mouth, he seemed to be clutching his oxygen mask to it. At this rate, he'd soon be in constant motion: perpetually switching from one to the other.

He reminisced about his childhood, how he hardly attended school, but on a rare day he did, once wore women's shoes. "We were too poor to buy any others," he said. At 13 he got his first conviction, for stealing a metal wheelbarrow. By 16 he was in Borstal, locked-up for thieving items including a speedometer and an oil pressure gauge.

"I went from crime to crime. Everyone I knew did. Receiving bent stuff. Selling bent stuff. There were no opportunities at all.

There was none of that 'Get on your bike and go out and get a fucking job.' It wasn't that easy." His gran had money, but squandered it. They used to go round to her place on Elgin Mews at Christmas and she'd give them a half a crown each.

His mum Daisy and younger brother Markie had emphysema like him, and both died fairly young. But his dad "drank like a fish and smoked like a train" and made it to 82. A dapper gambler rarely seen out of a suit, he was tough with them. Peter said he'd raised his children differently. Unlike his dad, he'd even cried in front of his kids. When his wife popped out, she planted a peck on his cheek, as did his grown-up son and daughter. "They all respect me," he said, beaming with pride when they left.

* * *

A few months later, I was back. In the background *Women Behind Bars*, about life inside a US high security jail, was showing on Sky's Crime and Investigation Network. "It's mostly coloureds in the prisons over there. They're racist. That lot are well fed though," Peter nodded towards the hefty black women waddling around a sports' field on the screen. The running commentary continued as the women belted out gospel songs with the fervour of the truly repentant. "They all believe in God. I did that. Went to church when I was inside. It helps when you go for parole."

As we watched, it became obvious he'd seen the programme before, particularly when he accurately foresaw that a woman jailed for killing her husband by poisoning his food would end up working in the prison kitchen. He soon admitted as much. Next on was *Cold Case Files*, about unsolved crimes in which criminals who thought they'd escaped justice were trapped by some vital piece of new evidence, like a DNA discovery.

As the evening wore on, Peter shared his brand of underworld wisdom and war stories, such as the time a white van was parked outside his house for what seemed forever. "My mate visited and kept on saying it was coppers watching me. I said, 'Don't be a cunt.' One day I went out and had a look, and gave the van a shake. I couldn't see anything." When the police arrested him, they said they'd had him under surveillance from the van for weeks.

"I always did my bird," he declared. The last time was 19 years ago when he was sentenced to nine months and ended up in Brixton. He didn't have to wear a uniform and the prison officers called him by his first name. The regime was too soft and he hated it. He shook his head, wistfully. "I preferred it before. It's all this do-gooders and civil rights now."

Crime itself had changed. "It was much safer then, I don't care what anybody says. You could walk the streets. There were fights every night, gangs really, but there were no muggings. We didn't even know what muggings were. We called it armed robbery. As you get older the next lot take over. You always get people coming up who are more dangerous than you. These blacks have gone absolutely potty today, killing each other. It's this respect game. They bump into each other and someone gets shot. It's all about territory. They're all youngsters."

As for the death penalty: "Don't let anyone tell you doing away with hanging stopped murders. When hanging was about, when we was on murder trial, I spoke to loads of gangsters and they said they wouldn't carry guns. Now they all do."

The trial he referred to was for the shooting of Billy Smith; a shooting that occurred one week before the first anniversary of the murder of Kelso Cochrane. If Kelso died because he was considered an alien, the same could never be said about Billy.

* * *

Hold tight, it's the Bells

Monday May 9, 1960. The hot evening was turning dark as a green mini-van with the name Turriff painted in white on its sides headed down Bramley Road, Notting Dale, and turned into Latimer Road.

Forty-six year old Ernie Bell was at the wheel. By day, he drove labourers between building sites. He'd fought in Burma during the war and had 10 convictions - all for 'selling liquor without a license and outside remitted hours'. With him were three of his sons and 'Little' Georgie Baker.

There was Peter, then 23-years-old. The week before he'd been bailed on charges of stealing a safe and its contents worth £25. There was Ernie junior, three years older than Peter, well-built, with fair-hair styled into a quiff, and married with two kids. There was Sydney, 18 years old and a former page boy at Claridge's who was now self-employed as a scrap dealer. And there was Georgie, a 24-year old painter with sharp features and thin lips. They were looking for Billy Smith, and knew where to find him.

At the junction of Latimer Road and Evesham Street, three men surrounded by oil rags and chippings were working on a Bedford lorry with maroon and blue paint showing through. They were, in a fashion, related.

Billy was scraping the paint off the side. He was wearing blue overalls, and was 21-years-old, 5ft 6in and whippet-thin. His 23-year-old cousin Nobby Buckingham toiled away underneath repairing a bumper, while Bill Cousins, pot-bellied and tattooed, put a spare wheel on the back. Cousins was Billy's unofficial step-dad.

The men were about to pack up. All of a sudden the Turriff van came into view. "Hold tight, it's the Bells," one of them said.

The van stopped in the middle of the road opposite the Trafalgar pub, and out jumped the Bells and Baker. They were armed with tools including a shovel, a chopper and a long piece of metal piping; the younger Ernie Bell had a rifle. Three of them went after Cousins, who ran down Evesham Street shouting: "Not me. It's nothing to do with me."

The younger Ernie Bell and Billy Smith stared into each other's eyes for a second. Seeing the gun, Billy's face turned ashen. He grabbed the sledgehammer he'd been changing the lorry's tyres with moments before. There are two accounts of what happened next:

The first, from various witnesses, has Billy throwing the hammer down, and then, with Ernie in pursuit, running into Latimer Road, turning right towards an alleyway leading to his aunt Nancy's house at number 115, but only making it 30 feet. "I told you we'd come," Ernie said. "See how brave you are now." Ernie raised the rifle to his right shoulder and fired.

The second, advanced later by Ernie Bell in his defence, has Billy throwing the 14lb sledgehammer at him, Ernie trying to avoid it, and the rifle going off in the process.

Either way, the outcome was the same. Billy fell to his knees, clutched his stomach with his right hand and, half crawling, forced his way up the side passage at the rear of the house. "Nancy, they've done me," he said.

Inside the living room his uncle Lawrence was watching *Wagon Train* on TV. The door was already open when Billy flopped in front him, groaning. At first Lawrence thought it was his son Rodney messing about. But turning on the light, he saw his nephew with blood seeping through his overalls. Lawrence called Nancy, who rushed in and then ran into the road crying. Rodney and some friends were standing opposite M. Gold and Co's metal factory. They'd witnessed the shooting from a distance of two feet.

One of them led Nancy back into the front room, where Billy was lying face down. The friend placed cushions under Billy's head and felt his pulse. It stopped, briefly revived, and then stopped completely. He put a mirror in front of Billy's mouth. It didn't cloud over. "He's gone," he said.

* * *

Norma Smith, a 19-year-old hairdressing assistant, told the *Daily Express* two days later that she and Billy had been saving every week for a white wedding and wanted to buy a hairdresser's shop "away from the back streets of Notting Hill". Her eyes were red with weeping, the paper said, and she fingered the diamond ring that Billy had bought her.

"I shall spend our savings on giving Billy the best funeral money can buy," she said.

"Billy was a very ordinary local boy who was trying to make good in the world. Everybody in the district liked him. And we were so much in love. He never got into trouble."

"We had been courting about 18 months when he was taken seriously ill. When he came out of hospital a couple of years ago my parents - who treated him just like their own son - asked him to live with us. He shared a bedroom with my brother Reggie."

"He hated rock 'n' roll, preferred songs by his favourite Mario Lanza. Tuesday was the pictures night. At weekends we went walking, or watched telly, or went for a quiet drink in the local."

* * *

Billy Smith's life had been tough from the start. His mum Kitty was one of 11 kids, and gave birth to him in Borstal when she was 17. She later worked in an electric factory and Billy was shunted around various addresses in Notting Dale. Kitty had another seven children before she died in 1952, when Billy was 14. Four of his siblings were in a children's home in Southend.

However, some say that he wasn't "the very ordinary" boy

the newspaper portrayed; that he was in fact someone who relished his growing reputation as one of the district's hard-nuts, and that this lay at the root of the feud which ultimately led to his death.

To understand one event in the Dale, so the story goes, you have to understand the ten events before it, and in turn, the ten events preceding each of those, and so on. In this case, hostilities between Billy and his mates on one side, and the Bells and Georgie Baker on the other, officially started less than two weeks before the shooting, with an insult to an old Irishman in a pub.

Friday April 22, 1960. The main venue in a saga of increasingly violent exchanges was The Latimer Arms, Billy's local on the corner of Walmer Road. A century before it had been a one-storied country inn. Now it was a not-especially rough pub with an outside toilet and three bars, where entertainment was provided by George on the piano and Danny on makeshift drums, which consisted of a hard chair and two beer bottles.

Billy was in the saloon bar drinking with friends, when Mick O'Donovan, an old Irish potman who'd worked there for nine years, walked by collecting glasses. "Irish bastard," said one of Billy's mates. The next time he walked by, the same young man kicked him on the leg. O'Donovan snapped and turned on him. The two men, with more than 40 years dividing them, had to be wrestled apart by the pub's landlord, and O'Donovan received a crack on the jaw.

Watching all this were Georgie Baker and Markie Bell, smaller than his absent older brothers Peter and Ernie. They confronted Billy and his mate, taking the old man's side. After a brief flare-up, tempers calmed and they all left.

Saturday April 30, 1960. The next instalment came the following week. Billy's friends were outside The Latimer Arms after closing time, when the younger Ernie Bell strolled over with Markie and Georgie Baker.

Ernie said he'd known O'Donovan a long time. "You took a

liberty last week, didn't you? You could have killed him like, being so old. The potman lost his job because of you. Everyone used to take the mickey out of him, but nobody ever hit him."

Billy's mate suggested settling it over on the Scrubs, meaning Wormwood Scrubs parkland by White City. There was pushing and shoving, then they went their separate ways.

Sunday May 1, 1960. The violence shifted up several notches. The setting, inevitably, was The Latimer Arms. The band was playing and the place was packed. Ernie called Billy to the centre of the saloon bar and prodded him in the chest with his finger. Then he pulled a handgun and put it to Billy's neck.

"I don't want guns you bastard," said Billy, jumping away. The drinkers near the door scrambled out to the street. Those trapped on the other side of the bar ducked. Ernie squeezed the trigger. Nothing happened.

Billy pulled out a long ivory-handled blade and lurched at Ernie, catching his groin and shoulder. Markie Bell ran at Billy with a bottle.

"Get back you little cunt," Billy shouted, "otherwise I'll break you in two."

Billy slashed out wildly, just missing Georgie Baker, but cutting Markie in his left arm.

Ernie later had five stitches in his shoulder and three in his groin. Markie's wound was much more severe. When a policeman came to take a statement from him at St Charles' Hospital, he refused to say who was responsible. "I saw a knife coming at me and stuck my arm up. If I get out of here alive I'll give this back to the bloke who done it, but it won't be in the arm," he said.

Monday May 2, 1960. At 10.45pm, Billy Smith and three friends drove round Notting Hill in a lorry. In Talbot Grove they saw Peter Bell sitting on the front steps talking to Georgie's younger sister Martha. The road was deserted. Billy pointed a shotgun out of the window at them, laughed, and pulled away.

Billy and his friends waited at the bottom of his street until about midnight for the trouble they expected. When it didn't show, he took the gun inside. "I don't think they'll come now. They'll swallow it," he said. Seven days later he was dead.

Wednesday June 29, 1960. After a two week Old Bailey trial, the jury returned their verdict in the case of Regina v Ernest William Bell the younger and others. Ernie junior had been charged with capital murder and faced the death penalty if convicted. The rest - Peter, Sydney, Ernest senior and Georgie Baker - were charged with non-capital murder, which carried a mandatory life sentence.

Ernie junior was found guilty of manslaughter, and jailed for seven years. Baker was also found guilty of manslaughter, on account of giving the loaded rifle to Ernie, and got five years. Peter, Sydney and their father were cleared of murder.

The Three Mrs Bells Weep with Joy said the *Daily Express*. "The past week has been the longest in our lives. Every day we waited and wondered, knowing the shadow of murder was over us," said Daisy Bell.

The police weren't celebrating. *"The result of this case was unsatisfactory particularly in view of the fact that a troublesome and violent family was involved,"* said an internal memo. *"The five accused men have all got criminal records and are well known in this area as persons who will resort to violence without the least hesitation especially when they are together."* It went on to highlight the peculiar challenge of investigating crime in Notting Hill: *"With the exception of the three young women, all of the eye witnesses to the shooting of Smith and the previous stabbing incidents were men with criminal records."* This was a neighbourhood where a code of 'see nothing, hear nothing' prevailed: *"The Bells knew that no one had told the police of the serious wounding of Mark Bell by stabbing; they know people in that area do not inform police of such feuds. Unfortunately this turned out to be a killing."* Buried within the same report, was a passage about the murder of Kelso Cochrane the year before, and a striking reference to the large number of people interviewed in both inquiries, and the police's grave suspicions about some of them.

* * *

On each visit I'd stayed several hours, with Peter puffing away on his roll-ups, as I drank endless cups of tea. He was greeting his deteriorating health with grim resolution.

After his heart attack he'd been given a pacemaker, and awoke from the operation gagging for a smoke. He stumbled out of bed, lit up, and crashed to the floor. They had to operate again. "The doctor said, 'That's never happened to me before.' I didn't tell him I'd just had a fag!"

He had already experienced death once. His heart stopped and everything went blank, that's why he didn't believe in an afterlife. "When you're gone, you're not coming back." If it wasn't for his family, he'd probably have ended it by now. "Every morning I wake up I wish I was dead. I hate being a burden. My head's right. I'm not scared."

He spoke of Billy Smith, how he'd known him all his life, how they went to Lancaster Road school together. "He was a mate, that's why he didn't shoot me when he drove by. Ernie admitted it. He did his time. I felt sorry for Georgie Baker, 'cos he was on his own...Afterwards everything settled down in the community. We all got together and decided we wouldn't go after anyone who gave evidence."

I'd handed him the old *Express* cutting about him and his friends searching for Kelso Cochrane's killer on my very first visit, and he'd studied the picture of his younger self with mild disbelief. I'd been upfront about what I was interested in from the start, but placed it among a range of subjects.

* * *

He was a teenager when the West Indians started arriving in greater numbers. "It was noticeable. We had them in our street. The government did it to keep the whites down," he said. "They did jobs you wouldn't do and all the wages went down. It's the same as now with the immigrants. Right now you can call up and get a cleaner for £5. The problem came because the rents used to be very low, but the blacks moved in and they went up. I knew Rachman. He was like that fucking what's his name, Van Hoogstraten. He had lots of people living in properties so the rents went up. Then the blacks tumbled it. It wasn't all streets paved with gold."

* * *

It was the one topic that all others had orbited around.

Do you think it was locals who killed Kelso Cochrane?

"Yes, I know it was." His blue eyes seemed to sparkle, not blinking. "Because I know who done it. But I'm not going to tell you, because he's still alive."

The killer didn't go on to be a career villain. He saw it as a fight, and he made what might have been a big mistake.

There was a party in Southam Street. They were all there. The killer returned to it and told everyone what he'd done. At that point he didn't know the man he'd stabbed had died. Around 40 people were at the party, but no one ever said a word.

Why not?

"They would have been killed."

I tried again, on another visit. Why did the police hold two people, Breagan and Digby, longer than anyone else?

"I knew you were going to ask that. Because any one of us could have done it. We all had form. We were there at the time. At the party."

But why those two in particular?

"They knew who did it."

I didn't say a word, just held his gaze...

It was dark and getting late. We talked about house prices and his garden. He shuffled slowly through the kitchen and we peered out of the back to take a look.

* * *

Copyright Mirrorpix.

"The worst-kept secret in Notting Hill"

He wouldn't speak on the record, but was happy to meet.

He was one of the many young men questioned about the murder, in his case for five hours. He knew Harrow Road station well, having been in some trouble over the years, and claimed the police back then would: "Give you a good kicking and happily take a bung".

Nowadays he spent his time giving lifts to old boys who needed driving to one place or another. It was his way of trying to compensate for some of the misery he'd caused in the past, he said.

At the mention of Kelso Cochrane, his heavy jowls creased into what looked like sympathy. He'd read that Kelso was a family man, he said. But he swore he had no idea who killed him. If it was locals, he said he definitely would have known.

He offered to take me around, show me how Notting Hill was in the old days. Over the next 18 months we'd meet, and on occasion drink at a working men's club where the prices and furnishings were from a bygone age. He was good company. One day he was driving and I was in the back of his car. He pointed out of the window. "That's where Southam Street was, where the party was…" Our eyes met in his rear view mirror.

"It was diabolical what happened. I'm telling you now, but I'll always deny it. It was a racist killing."

And the perpetrator?

"It's the worst-kept secret in Notting Hill."

CHAPTER SIX

AN UNEXPECTED CALLER

Susie told Brian about it early in their relationship. She knew it would come up one day, she said, but didn't know how. So when it finally resurfaced early one evening in April 2006, she believed it was somehow fated.

It was their usual Saturday ritual: after getting in the weekly shopping at Tesco, the couple drove home, unpacked it, then Brian switched on the telly and settled down while his wife changed into the comfy blue kaftan she wore around the house. Normally she marked off the programmes she wanted to watch in the *Radio Times*, but this week she hadn't. So it was a stroke of luck when BBC Two came straight on and an old black man appeared in a cemetery on a winter's day. He was brushing away layers of dirt from a gravestone. The dirt was so encrusted that at first the name on the slab was obscured, but as a strong acid was poured over it and the man swept away with a broom, the words became clear.

"Kelso Cochrane 1927 – 1959. From the Trades Council and his West Indian Friends."

The old man had a moustache and glasses, and was wearing a peaked winter hat and a smart black coat. Afterwards he sat down on a bench to be interviewed. "This is the first time I personally have been able to make some contribution to my brother's burial," said Stanley Cochrane. "I wanted to put closure to what's haunting me and my other relatives because nobody's ever been arrested...It's not possible to have peace of mind because the murderer is still out there. The police are sort of dormant right now on this case. But I'm sure hoping they will keep an open mind on this matter."

As he watched the screen, Brian shouted to his wife in the bedroom. "Sue, you better get in here." At first, she ignored him. The programme was almost over. "Sue, get in here," he yelled, raising his voice. She ambled into the front room.

"What did you say that bloke's name was? Oslo?" he asked.

"Well, it's not Oslo. It's Kelso."

"Quick, get a video in," said Susie.

Brian fumbled around for a cassette and got the recorder going. Then they watched the final minutes together. Afterwards Susie turned to him and said: "Christ. I knew I wasn't imagining it." A few days later, she wrote to the BBC.

* * *

Susie Read lived in a spotless bungalow in the middle of England, reached after a journey along twisting country lanes which cut through rolling green fields. It had been decades since she'd left Notting Hill, but the place remained in her vowels and turns of phrase, in her plain speaking and willingness to put the kettle on and offer endless cups of tea.

She claimed to know something about the murder. Something she hoped could make a difference. But it was so intricately woven into her own story that the two had to be unravelled together, and it was best to start at the beginning, with her childhood in a tenement on Kenley Street, a Dale slum street that had disappeared long ago.

On the surface, her upbringing was perfectly ordinary for the time and the place: the outdoor loo, sleeping top-to-tail with her sister in the same bed, washing in a tin bath with water boiled in a saucepan, her mum shoving malt down her throat three times a week, and Nitty Norah pouring stinking liquid on her scalp and rummaging through her locks for lice at primary school. Everyone knew everyone else's business, you never grassed on your mates, and you could set your watch by the arrival of the rag and bone man.

Eight hundred yards from her front door was the most notorious address in the country - 10 Rillington Place - and she grew up hearing tales of the monster who had recently lived there. John Reginald Halliday Christie was an upstanding member of the community and a special constable at Harrow Road police station during the war. He was also a necrophiliac who murdered at least six women, hiding their remains around his grotty little home near Ladbroke Grove tube station. His barely literate housemate Timothy Evans was hanged for murder - protesting his innocence to the end - before a West Indian tenant stumbled across a body in a sealed alcove in the kitchen soon after moving in, and justice finally closed in on the bald, bespectacled Christie. Locals likened him to Jack the Ripper, and described his victims with callous disregard. "Why worry?" Susie would hear them say. "They were only brasses."

Holland Park Comprehensive opened the week after the Notting Hill riots, and she started the following year, cycling up the hill every morning to the modern building with glass-covered walkways surrounded by international embassies and a park with exotic peacocks - which she'd feed in her breaks with bits of bread she'd nicked from home. The so-called Socialist Eton was an experiment in classless education, its intake reflecting the wildly varying fortunes of the area's residents. Poor, white kids like her found themselves sitting next to the offspring of West Indian immigrants, as well as children with double-barrel surnames, born of the liberal intelligentsia from Holland Park's mansions. "Rough. Smooth. Black. White. We all got on. But we didn't mix outside," Susie recalled.

All this was normal for a girl growing up in Notting Dale. Yet at home it was a different story.

People always said that Susie was the spitting image of her mum, Pat Read: both naturally petite, with the same brown eyes and fine dark brown hair (though Pat dyed hers blonde), the same bone structure, even the same facial expressions. "If you look at me, you see her," she said. But their relationship was uneasy, complicated by the times Pat put Susie and one of her brothers into children's homes because she said she couldn't cope; distorted also, by Susie's relationships with the men her mum took up with - the men who at different times and in different ways, took the role of father in Susie's life.

First, there was her real dad, Harry Read, about whom she had little to say, and none of it good. "He used to beat me with a horsewhip and lock me in the cupboard. He was mentally insane, a manic depressive. My mum could have stopped it, but never did." When Susie was about six he left, and she'd hardly seen him since.

Jingles came next. Even now, barely a week passed without him entering her thoughts. "I was Jingles' little girl and he was my God. As far I'm concerned he was my dad." Since Jingles was black, no-one would have mistaken him as such - particularly not the kids at school who she fought when they said he wasn't. Susie remembered the abuse that followed the couple when they were out, like the white woman who came up to them in the street, spat in her mum's face and said: "You're nothing but a dirty old whore going with the spade."

When Jingles - "a gentleman" who was "always smartly dressed" and "had pearls for teeth" - was going out, he'd often take Susie along, usually to a black club on Westbourne Park Road, where she drank orange juice from white plastic cups while the men sat on rickety chairs playing dominoes. They all knew her. "Sometimes I'd annoy the old boys, turning their dominoes over if they got up to use the bathroom. I was full of mischief, but never got told off as such." It was there that she saw Jingles lose his cool for the only time. "A man swore in front of me and Jingles wasn't having it. He slapped the fag straight out of his hand."

All of a sudden, Jingles was gone from her life, leaving in his wake a mystery Susie still hoped to resolve decades on. It had been the subject of furtive gossip in a home that was bursting with secrets: where conversations stopped in their tracks when she walked into the room, and where Susie would sit, hovering on the stairs, straining to hear things she wasn't supposed to.

"One minute my mum had a bump. Then she didn't. It was all covered up. I heard so many stories. That she had the baby aborted. That she had it adopted. Another that Jingles had taken it." She'd written to the TV show *Trisha* to see if its researchers could discover whether she had a half-brother or sister out there somewhere, but heard nothing. Her mum had died years ago, and wouldn't have told her anyway, and Jingles was the only name she ever knew him by, and she hadn't a clue where or how her mum met him, or even if he was still alive, so she didn't know what else she could do.

There was, she believed, an overlap between Jingles' departure and the arrival of her mum's final partner, the man Pat Read was with for close to a quarter of a century. "They used to call them the two Pats. She was besotted by him. She was a lot older and he was her toy boy. He would have been a prize catch, the local catch, and she always told everyone what a good-looking devil he was. Love is as love does I suppose."

Pat Digby had dark blonde hair, tattoos on his hands and lived just around the corner, opposite the Prince of Wales pub on Princedale Road, in a house with a big art deco mirror on the wall in the main room, a white budgie in the kitchen and chickens in the back yard. Before Pat moved in with them, before they all left Notting Dale, moving first to Burnt Oak and then eventually further west to Hillingdon, Susie would go round there to see his mum, Emily. "I loved to brush her hair. She always kept it in a bun and when she untied it, it came to her waist. Her hands put you in mind of a very frail old lady. I think she had arthritis in one arm. She was a matriarch, as most from that area were, and a bit strict, but she was a lovely woman. Pat was her little soldier. I don't think he could do anything wrong as far as she was concerned."

Digby had been in and out of the Merchant Navy, signing up as a steward when he was 17, travelling the world on Norwegian and British vessels. For a while, he had a little spider monkey that he'd apparently acquired on one trip, which would sit on his shoulder and snarl if people got too close. Many of his friends went on to be career criminals, but not him: he worked as a painter and decorator, mostly cash in hand, and lived beneath the radar. Every now and then, said Susie, a letter would come from the tax people, or there would be a knock at the door, but he'd rip them up, or her mum would tell the caller she'd never heard of him.

"I'll give him his due, he always worked. It always amazed me how he could drive home drunk at three in the morning, literally fall through the door and stagger into bed fully clothed. You'd hear him snoring then he'd wake up for work at five o'clock. No alarm clock. Nothing." He would give her mum cash every week, but mostly he drank what he earned, surviving his hangovers by knocking back Bombay Oysters: a vile mix of raw eggs in milk, vinegar and water. It was the one thing Susie had learned from him that she still put to good effect.

He reminded her somehow of the wily Lee Marvin character in *Paint Your Wagon*. "He'd make out he's a fool, but he isn't. He's as sharp as a tack." "Everything was always a grin", and while "he had lots of friends, he didn't really seem to trust any of them". He wasn't political. "Unless Labour got in and put a penny on a pint, and then they would be the biggest scum of the earth." He loved his documentaries. "*Panorama, World in Action*, he'd watch them all. You couldn't talk while they were on." He collected true crime magazines. "He built up his collection, and kept them all neat in folders." He doted on the family dog Cindy, a Collie mixed with Alsatian, who he brought home one day as a tiny puppy tucked under his coat. "He said he saw it on the side of the road, but I still think he nicked it to this day."

Her mum, she believed, put him before her kids. "I don't think he could do anything wrong as far as she was concerned, the same way his mother was with him...She'd get him steak and we'd have egg and chips 'cos she couldn't afford to get us meat as well. He got the best of everything and we'd get the scraps."

The two Pats would "party at the drop of a hat", but preferred she wasn't there when they did. "I was always the one they wanted out of the way, probably because I was rebellious, the bolshie one who answered back. But if you played the fool you could stay, and I played the fool. It was me who always started the singing - Connie Francis and Brenda Lee songs. They'd love all that. And like in *Oliver Twist* when Nancy pretends to Fagin she's more drunk than she is, I'd pretend to be a helluva lot more pissed than I was."

Susie was blunt about how much she hated him, how on edge she was when he was around, how volatile their relationship was. "When he was out, I'd listen for the key in the front door, thinking 'Is it all going to kick off?' If he hadn't been in a punch-up, he'd come in and pick on me. If he was in a good mood I'd try my best to keep it going. If he was pissed I'd give him another drink, hoping he'd pass out. You didn't dare have an opinion when he was there and when he left you'd say I'd say I'm glad that bastard's gone, but never openly."

"You'd have to live with him to really know him. To the outside world he presents himself as a pillar of society, and if you met him in a pub, you'd say, 'What a nice guy'. But he always had something to prove. He could turn on a sixpence and pack a punch when he'd had a few." He had two catchphrases: "If I'd had a gun I would've shot him" and "Let them hang" - usually directed at someone on the TV who'd made his blood boil.

Pat Digby, she acknowledged, did treat her aunt's disabled son well, and always ensured that Freddie Willis, an old boy who came round to their house and ended up twice as drunk as anyone else, got home safely - but, as far as she was concerned, that was about it. "He's hard to fathom. He's got no fear, no fear at all. You could think he's your best friend but at the same time he's stabbing you in the back." Then there were his views on black people.

"He was over-the-top racist. The stupid thing was in his later years he'd work with black blokes and he was all over them like a fly. Now this is how his mind works. He loved Muhammed Ali. Unless he beat Henry Cooper, then he was the biggest coon going, and it was, 'Go on Henry, smash his black face in.' I mean, I like Bob Marley, UB40, all that. But if you played those records, he'd come in and break them. You wouldn't have dared say that you liked a black group. But then I remember saying something about Stevie Wonder, a stupid joke that was going round, and he actually said what a good artist he was. Whether that was just a good day or not, I don't know."

When Susie's niece married a black Baptist minister, Pat Read fretted. "I said to my sister, 'Blimey, what's Digby going to say?' I was frightened. But you wouldn't have thought he was the same man. If we were going to see them he'd always try to get out of it. But if he went there he was the nicest person on the face of the earth."

Naturally, no one dared utter Jingles' name within his earshot. But when he argued with her mum, he'd sometimes throw it in her face, calling her a "fucking nigger lover" - as if the thought of them together was the most repulsive thing on earth. Jingles wasn't the only black man whose name wasn't welcome in their home.

For as long as Susie could remember, she'd been aware of it. Sometimes she understood the name to be Elso or Oslo. Whatever it was, it lurked in the shadows, like rumours of her mum's pregnancy. Every so often, it was dragged into the open.

One such time was on July 2, 1967, she remembered the date because it was her 18th birthday. During the day, the two Pats bought Susie a dress in Edgware, which looked like something out of *Pride and Prejudice*, and in the evening friends gathered at their home in Burnt Oak for a booze-up. "It was join in or get ignored. We were in the front room and everyone was drinking. One of his mates brought up a murder and said the name Kelso. The blood literally drained from Digby's face and he looked at us kids to see if we'd clocked it."

Then there was the occasion something came on the TV about a black man being killed, she couldn't exactly recall when. "Digby said: 'Thank God for that. Another fucker gone.' One of his mates turned to him and said: 'Well you got away with it Diggo.'" Digby looked round, and speaking through gritted teeth, said: "Shut your mouth, you don't know what you're talking about."

There were similar incidents, she claimed, usually when his friends were there and the alcohol was flowing. Someone would mention Kelso, Digby would seem to tense and mutter some sort of denial. "I would always think, "Why did you bring them home, you stupid...because drink loosens tongues."

A couple of years before Digby finally left her mum, Susie confronted him directly about 'Elso'.

It was a warm day. The back door was open. Pat rolled in from the pub and immediately he and Susie were at each other's throats in the kitchen. "He was always in the mood for a punch-up unless people were there. If there were five of us in the room, he'd make straight for me: '*You slut, you effing this...*' I can't remember what it was over. All it needed was spilt tea and it would be world war three. He started prodding me and I said, 'Don't start Pat. I'm not in the mood.' Probably one of my brave days. Or stupid days. He hit me and I threw something at him."

Before she knew it, they were outside, tearing into one another, tumbling through the rockery halfway up her mum's garden. "I stuck my fingers into his eyes trying to poke them out. There was a lot of blood."

"He said: 'Get off me you bitch, or I'll kill you.' And I said: 'Like you killed Elso.'"

Susie repeated it; again and again. "You did kill him. Didn't you? You murdering bastard."

Then, she claimed, Digby admitted it: "Yeah. So what if I did. You can't prove nothing."

* * *

So this was Susie's story: it was more than hearsay, it was an alleged confession. Looking back now, in some warped way, perhaps to taunt her, she thought part of him always wanted her to know. "It sounds strange, but he did and he didn't, if you know what I mean." Yet under the glare of a court-room cross-examination, her story would be vulnerable on various fronts.

First, how long she'd taken to come forward. In response, she said that she feared Digby might harm her mum while she was alive. Moreover, she worried that no-one would believe her. She'd once had a breakdown and her mum had convinced everyone that she was "a nutter". But seeing "that man's brother on the telly" had moved her. What's more, one of her best friends had been stabbed in the leg recently by a gang of youths, so when it came to 'Elso', she knew she couldn't look away and bury it forever. "For years I've held it in, but you can only go through life closing your eyes for so long."

Second, there was the confession itself. An admission during a fight in which she tried to gouge his eyes out twenty years ago wasn't exactly evidentially overwhelming. Throw in her professed hatred of him, and the fact that although her life now was a model of order, her past was chaotic, and a competent defence lawyer could tear her testimony apart.

Yet Susie Read was unwavering: "I know for a fact he's done it, 'cos he admitted it." She didn't want publicity or money. She just wanted Pat Digby in jail.

* * *

After their fight, she only saw him a few times. When she visited her mum, it was on the understanding that he wasn't around. Then Pat Digby left Pat Read for another woman. "My mum was broken-hearted. I still believe she loved him till the day she died. She often used to say she wanted to find out where he lived and go and hit the woman. Or that she was going to tell her all about his past."

* * *

Autumn 2006. The day was dull and overcast as Susie walked with a pounding heart up to the bungalow at the end of the little cul-de-sac. As she reached the back door, she saw him at the kitchen window.

"Blimey. It's Susan," Digby said, the astonishment written on his face.

He opened the door before she even rang the bell. His beard was greyer, his stomach heavier, otherwise he hadn't changed a bit in the 18 years since she'd laid eyes on him.

Overcome by anxiety, Susie immediately started crying. "Oh Digby, I've got to see you. These people have turned up at my door." She showed him a letter from the BBC asking about the murder and what she knew about Pat Digby. The letter was a sting, designed to draw him out.

His partner, a well-preserved woman in her sixties, joined them. Digby read the letter dismissively.

"How did you find me?" he asked.

"You're in the phone book."

"No I ain't."

His partner piped up: "Yes you are Pat."

Susie turned to her. "It's ok. We parted on bad terms, but hopefully now there's no bad feelings, hey Pat? We always had

Pat Digby in 1966.

punch-ups Pat, didn't we? We was always having rucks and arguments."

He offered her a cup of tea and a little dog came running in. Susie used its entrance to gather her thoughts, leaning down and fussing over it as she tried to gain composure. "I've just lost my dog Lucky," she said.

Digby's partner took the letter and studied it with mounting anger. "I'll get a stop to this," she said.

Susie suggested going into the front room, and turned and moved towards it, before realising the couple weren't following. All the while she thought about the Samurai swords Digby hung on the walls wherever they lived. She had a vision of him coming at her with one of them.

But Digby didn't move from the kitchen window. He kept glancing out of it, as if he was expecting something else to happen.

"Did you know mum died?" Susie asked.

"No."

"Yeah, she's been dead about six years."

It had been about ten minutes, and he'd said nothing in any way incriminating. Susie said she had to go, and went towards the door. He ran his hand up and down her back, like he was looking for something. He put his arm round her and kissed her cheek. As she left, the dog ran out behind her.

A couple of weeks later, Susie phoned him.

"You did it, didn't you?"

"I don't know what you're on about," he replied.

"You did Digby. 'Cos you admitted it to me."

He went quiet for a second. "I've got nothing else to say."

"You're a liar and you know it."

* * *

May 2007. Jingles' old Jamaican friend was worried why I was looking into him. "He was a good man," he said. "He wasn't involved in any shady business." He spelt out his surname: "D. R. A. G. G. O. N."

Jingles, it turned out, had died in 1993 aged 60. He was originally from Montego Bay, had lived in Colville Terrace, and worked as a chef. It was an unusual name, so tracing his relatives didn't take long. I sent out letters to half-a-dozen of them. Perhaps one could solve the mystery of Pat Read's pregnancy.

A single response, by way of a phone call, came a few days later. A female operator explained that this was an assisted call, that the person on the other end had speech difficulties and would type their messages, which she would then read. At the end of each passage of dialogue, the operator would say 'Go ahead'. I should do the same. It made for an oddly disjointed conversation.

"You wrote..." pause...*"to me about Mr Draggon..."* pause...*"Go ahead."*

"Yes. I was trying to get some information. Did you know him? Go ahead."

"He was..." pause...*"my dad. Go ahead."*

"I was trying to find out about a lady he used to know. Her name was Pat Read. Go ahead."

"She was..." pause…*"my mum. Do you know..."* pause...*"if she's still alive?..."* pause…*"Go ahead."*

The caller, it emerged, was a 45-year-old woman with cerebral palsy. She'd been abandoned at birth by Pat Read, and though Jingles had maintained contact, bringing her to Notting Hill at weekends and taking her out with him to local pubs, she'd spent most of her life in care. She greeted the news cautiously that she had a half-sister, Susie, who would love to meet her.

* * *

Some Day

"It is in justice that the ordering of society is centred,"
Aristotle.

Saturday May 16, 2009. Fifty years after violence erupted on the
streets of Notting Hill - the time of shattered windows, broken
limbs and cries of "Go home you black bastards" filling the air -
a series of events was held in the district commemorating the
1958 race riots. They ended ten months later, exactly half a
century after Kelso Cochrane's murder.

So it was that at noon on a blustery Saturday, around 70
people gathered by his grave in Kensal Green Cemetery. All those
summers before, 1,000 mourners had squeezed together here,
some scaling the wall behind to get a clear view, as the Rev
Ronald Campbell, chaplain to the West Indians in Great Britain,
led a short service. Olivia Ellington stood at the front and Det
Supt Forbes-Leith looked on, as the coffin was lowered into the
earth and people surged forward, only to be held back by
stewards. For an hour afterwards hundreds had remained,
singing hymns with "deeply emotional emphasis", said *The
Times*.

Between 1960, and the laying of the Portland stone slab that
Kelso's fellow West Indian carpenter Randolph Beresford raised
the money for, and 2005, when Stanley Cochrane scrubbed it
clean with potent muriatic acid while in England trying to get
justice for his brother, the grave had fallen into neglect. Now, two
gleaming, intricately-crafted mosaics covered it. One showed
Kelso's standard bespectacled image; the other Antigua and
Barbuda's national flag, beneath his name and lifespan.

The new memorial was the brainchild of Eddie Adams, a trade
unionist with a silver quiff and amiable manner, who had lived in

Notting Hill all his life. In 1959, and a member of the Youth Communist League, he'd stood and watched on Ladbroke Grove as Kelso's cortège passed by.

Adams mounted a small step-ladder by the grave, and began the introductions in a soft voice. Before him were a mix of locals and activists, some recording the event for posterity on video cameras and mobile phones. Someone shouted "Speak up", but Adams finished quickly, and Suresh Grover, a veteran anti-racist campaigner in a grey suit with crumpled trousers, stepped forward. Many had fallen since Kelso in similar circumstances, Grover said, reeling off names. *Blair Peach. Joy Gardner. Zahid Mubarek. Stephen Lawrence.*

A slim young black man with a serious air walked up. Duwayne Brooks was Stephen Lawrence's friend, and was with him on the night of April 22, 1993, when a white gang attacked and murdered him. Growing up, Brooks said, he'd been told lightning never struck twice in the same place. Yet Kelso Cochrane and Stephen Lawrence proved this wrong. "In Kelso's case the police *refused* to accept it was a racist murder, and said it was a robbery. In Stephen's case they *refused* to accept it was a racist murder. I know what it's like not to get justice from the system...Those who committed this murder lived their lives because of the failure of the police."

A volley of applause was followed by the appearance of David Neita, a tall poet with a shock of honey-coloured locks who delivered his verse in a rich Jamaican baritone:

"...Bob Marley asked us how long shall they kill our prophets?

We also ask: how long shall they kill our architects, like Stephen Lawrence?

How long shall they kill our soldiers, like Christopher Alder?

How long shall they kill our lawyers, like Kelso Cochrane?"

A local councillor and singers with especially written songs came and went. As did Gerry Gable. With his moustache and trilby, he would have done well in an Inspector Clouseau look-alike contest. In fact he was the nemesis of generations of British fascists, compulsively tracking their activities since the early 60s, and once receiving a letter bomb for his efforts.

Gable spoke of the BNP threat in the forthcoming European elections. Then he offered his theory on Kelso's murder. "I was very happy three weeks ago to be writing obituaries for Colin Jordan who ran the White Defence League in this area. People make the mistake of thinking it was Mosleyites who killed that lad [Kelso]. I don't think so. I think they were Jordan's storm troopers, Spearhead, that he eventually got sent to prison for. These people are savages and are not fit to be in any society." The Godfather of British Fascism had died at the age of 85 on April 9, 2009, living his last years in a remote farmhouse in the Yorkshire Dales, certain of his Aryan superiority to the end.

The speeches over, people assembled to march down Ladbroke Grove, echoing the procession of 50 years before in the opposite direction. They filed through the triumphal arch at the front of cemetery, walked the short distance to the corner of Harrow Road and turned into Ladbroke Grove, where they were hit by a downpour. Buffeted by the wind and rain, they passed the Saturday shoppers heading into Sainsbury's on the right and proceeded down the road's gradual decline. The pavement had overflowed as their forebears accompanied the coffin up to Kensal Green. Now a small group huddling under the 52 bus stop looked on in mild bemusement. Trailing a few feet behind everyone was an old black lady whose spine was so curved she was almost bent double. In her hand was a placard creatively fashioned out of a Foxton's letting sign with Kelso's picture plastered over the estate agent's details.

Sunday May 17, 2009. The next afternoon many of the same faces were back among the crowd collecting outside The Grove Bar and Restaurant, a gastro-pub on the corner of Golborne Road. A steel pan band played sunny rhythms from the pavement as people sheltered beneath their umbrellas, anticipating more rain.

This was once the Earl of Warwick, and on his tour of the district before announcing his candidacy in the 1959 General Election, Sir Oswald Mosley had been greeted here with a rousing rendition of "For he's a jolly good fellow". Seven months later, on the night of the murder, there'd been a whip-round, invites were handed out, and bottles carried the two hundred yards to Ma O'Brien's party, where the drinking continued in the front room on the ground floor. The following day, Arthur Cook of the *Daily Mail* visited the pub and heard Nora the pianist play the favourites as an old woman took round a hat, and people spoke with dread about what would happen next.

Looking around, the past wasn't quite a foreign country. The old iron bridge Kelso had stumbled towards after being attacked was still there, rusting and plastered in graffiti tags and scraps of advertising. Beneath it ran the railway tracks which the police had combed for the murder weapon, and the Heathrow Express now shot by on. Thirty yards along Golborne Road there was no trace of The Mitre, the pub seven youths emerged from on the night of the killing to abuse a passing black stranger. It had burnt down in mysterious circumstances decades ago, and in its place was a bustling Portuguese café, where people sat outside on warm days drinking galão coffees. A little further down an old chapel and hostel for homeless ex-prisoners had been converted into a studio for Stella McCartney's swanky fashion label. Opposite was a Moroccan stall selling freshly grilled fish, and next door a halal butcher. Just beyond it, on the other side of the street, was Bevington Road: where Kelso had left, but never made it back to that night.

What of Southam Street, scene of Ma O'Brien's celebration, where the killer supposedly returned and blurted out what he'd just done?

Apart from one little stretch, that too was gone: declared unfit for human habitation by the council in 1963 and demolished six years later. Now the skyline was dominated by thirty-one storeys of concrete. For years, Trellick Tower was known as Colditz in the Sky - and notorious for muggings, broken lifts, discarded needles, and hallways where the smell of disinfectant never quite erased the stink of urine. But as gentrification had inched its way northwards, into even this corner of the borough, the tower block's reputation had been transformed. Now it was an English Heritage listed building, some of its flats sold to rich private tenants, and advertised as edgy dwellings with stunning views in a desirable postcode.

A black car pulled up by the pub and the children of James Christian - Kelso's best friend and cousin, who had identified his body the morning after he was killed - emerged with their mother Rose. She'd come straight from the airport where she'd flown in from Antigua. After handshakes and introductions everyone bunched in as Jak Beula, a snappily-dressed man from a trust promoting black history, took the microphone. Beula gestured to the pavement beneath him - just across the road from where Kelso was attacked and fell - and said: "[Kelso Cochrane] died on this spot, on this place exactly 50 years ago..."

"Yes brother!" hollered an old black man.

"Kelso's body may be a shell, but his spirit lives on through his family," Beula continued. Then he urged the crowd to chant Kelso's name three times.

"Kelso Cochrane. Kelso Cochrane. Kelso..." On the final shout, the Mayor of Kensington and Chelsea pulled a purple rope to reveal a blue plaque, which read:

"Kelso Cochrane. 1927 - 1959. Antiguan carpenter was fatally stabbed on this site. His death outraged and unified the community leading to the lasting cosmopolitan tradition in North Kensington."

Rose Christian, a few weeks shy of her eightieth birthday, lifted her glasses and dabbed her eyes. Her husband's grief had never left him. Up to his death in 2003, she would find James sitting in silent contemplation, his eyes welling up. "When I lost Kelso," he would say, "it was like losing myself." The Antiguan High Commissioner placed a comforting arm around her. His words could just be overhead. "Don't worry" he was saying. "Some day."

In the bar afterwards, music played, people drank, and - stirred by the emotion of it all - talk turned to resurrecting the case. Perhaps this was the last chance?

Over the following weeks emails flowed discussing how to get "Justice for Kelso". Was there a "collective stomach for a fight" asked one. It appeared there was, but the Antiguan community and the dead man's family would have to be included, it was decided. A Freedom of Information request for the murder case files was submitted, but it was summarily refused. *"There remains a possibility, however remote, that this case could be re-opened for re-investigation at some point in the future,"* came the reply. *"It is not in the public interest to jeopardise a prosecution for murder by releasing information that could be of later significance".*

The campaigners then learned that Stanley Cochrane had already got the police to re-open the case in 2003, and pushed things as far as he could. Their nascent campaign was over.

CHAPTER SEVEN

LET IT LIE

His name meant nothing to the bemused Bengali woman who opened the door at the address that the electoral roll threw up for him. But I later found out that he was living in north west London, apparently on an estate by a little park, where he was often seen whiling away the hours on a bench. One still autumn morning I went there, and not having his exact address, approached every old man who entered, asking if they were Frank, or perhaps knew him. None did. Then I trudged around the estate, back and forth among the uniform rows of four-storey concrete blocks, asking passers-by the same question, and drawing only blanks. It was the same at the local betting shops and pubs.

The coldest winter for 30 years set in, and it looked like somebody else who may have been able to unlock the past had disappeared into the ether. He'd been in the vicinity on the night of the murder, was one of the dozens of young men swept up by the police and questioned at Harrow Road in the days afterwards, and his name cropped up here and there as someone worth speaking to. Finally, with Spring in the air, and the streets full of pink flesh being exposed to sunlight for the first time in months, I found him.

"Oh, Frank, he's just come in", said the African caretaker at the estate, shaking his head with the affection reserved for a local character.

He led me to a block at the back. Frank was on the balcony, his key in the door, about to open it. A slight man with a pallid complexion - who didn't want to talk. It had taken months to find him. Within five minutes he'd turned, shut the door and gone. I dropped him a letter a few days later and he called me back.

* * *

"It's a miserable old place. You can't hear a soul out there." Frank gestured to the window. His living room felt like a fraying hospital lounge: the ancient little telly, the tatty straw chair a neighbour had left and never picked up, a faint whiff of stale cigarette smoke. "Normally where you live you can hear kids in the distance, and then a little bit further down you can hear people talking to each other. But here it's unbelievable. It just goes *dead*. Occasionally you hear a telephone ring. I've got to get out."

At night though, the silence was shattered by his neighbour. "She comes out without a stitch on and stands on the balcony screaming and shouting. It's not her fault, poor cow. She's doolally. I tell her carer when he comes, but he always says: 'She wouldn't do that'."

Lately he'd been feeling low. "I was talking to a bloke and he said, 'Depression's worse than cancer because it takes everything away from you'. So I've been doing these big long walks. This morning I got out and I felt it lifting. I felt it going away. It was fantastic. I thought 'Thank God for that'. It's to do with the sun. Vitamin D."

The estate may have been dead, but it wasn't safe. He said a young man had barged his way into his flat just as he was opening the door a few months ago. They'd grappled on the couch, before the intruder ran off with his wallet which contained the cash he'd been saving for a new TV.

"I'm *very* anti-thieving now." He smiled, acknowledging his own youthful history of petty crime. "Funny how you change. If anyone says, 'Oh, he's a thief'. I say, 'He's a horrible fucking person, get away from me. I don't want to know you.' Once they stand over your door, that's wrong. They've taken away your freedom. When I leave here, I make sure every window's locked, even if it's a boiling hot day."

His view of growing up in Notting Dale, unusually, wasn't drenched in nostalgia. "It wasn't as fantastic as that. People were always falling out. It wasn't all Robin Hood. Look at what's his name" - a well-known local former armed robber - "used to pretend he was a big gangster, but he done my mother's gas meter."

Now they were a vanishing generation. "My God, they're all dead. They're all *dead*." And those who were still around all seemed to have been struck by some terrible affliction or another. "They all ended up with sicknesses, diseases, walking sticks. It wasn't a straightforward retirement." The other day he'd seen one of Rachman's old henchmen going around the park in an electric wheelchair. Once he placed fear in the hearts of the tenants he terrorised on behalf of the most infamous landlord in history. Now the pigeons barely got out of his way. "Another bloke yesterday, I just took one look at him. His teeth are all black stumps. And he used to be so immaculate." Every time he went to the GP's surgery, Frank ran into someone who'd tell him of a mutual acquaintance who was gone. "I wish they wouldn't. That's all you want."

"It was my birthday yesterday. How old do you think? Tell the truth."

68.

"69. Still going."

Two white feathers fluttered onto the beige carpet in the centre of the room. "That Gloria Hunniford's daughter, she said whenever she saw a feather it was an angel come to see her. She said they helped her with her illness. Her cancer. She was always finding them. I don't believe in it myself. But if they started falling all around me I would. Bloody hell."

* * *

"Anything I can answer, I'll answer."

I'd moved gently towards it, but the subject raised itself.

Frank remembered the night of Saturday, May 16, 1959 well. He'd been at the wedding. A few of them went on to Ma O'Brien's party afterwards, but not him. "One lot went that way down the road. We went the other." The next morning he was at home reading the *News of the World* in bed when the CID arrived and told him - just like in the old movie cliché: "Don't plan on going away any time soon".

"I could never figure out why the police never opened up that case again. Maybe his brother [Stanley] couldn't afford to come back again. He scraped together the money the first time he came, but he didn't have a pot to piss in. He said, 'I've got to go back, I can't do any more.'"

How would locals have reacted if a young white man from the area had been sentenced to hang for the murder?

"It would have gone crazy."

"Pat Digby." He says the name, unprompted. "I wonder if he's still alive?"

They grew up together. Of all the lads, Pat was the one the local girls swooned over, the first one to have a pair of blue jeans, which he'd bought on one of his Merchant Navy trips. Digby liked hanging around villains, "but wasn't one himself". He was a bit of a coward if truth be told, Frank said.

On a later visit, Frank opened up more.

That Sunday after the murder, after the police had visited, he said he was with Digby at the end of Portland Road. They were tossing pennies in the air, betting which way they would land. "We were talking, standing there playing 'two ups'. He was playing with us and he's killed a bloke the night before. He told me he'd done it and they'd never get him. A bloke said to me recently, that where he hid the knife, it's still there."

Where's that?

"Well, it doesn't take much working it out, does it? A bloke's

137

dead. A black bloke's lying dead. What the police were doing, nobody knows. 'Cos he was a black bloke, a black person - '*What you want to worry about him for? Just let it lie*' - that all come into it. So naturally it doesn't take much to work out. He lives with his mum. That's the first thing you do when you're wanted by the police, you go home. You shouldn't. You should go somewhere else, but you hit for home. He hit for home. Now, in them days where do you hide a knife? You'd hide it under the floorboards, don't you? That's all you got to think. They might have done all the houses up, modernised them and made them posh, but did they rip the floorboards up? Did they say: 'We'll just nail the floorboards down, put a bit of carpet on it.' It's straightforward isn't it? What's that Sherlock Holmes says? Elementary."

* * *

The blinds were drawn at 74 Princedale Road, Colin Jordan's old headquarters. Two generations before, wire mesh covered the windows and White Defence League was daubed in big, bold letters across the front. In 1963 protestors showered the building with eggs and bottles, while inside Jordan and the French perfume heiress Françoise Dior celebrated their marriage by cutting their ring fingers, and letting their mingled blood fall on an open page of *Mein Kampf*.

Had Jordan sold the place recently, the fascist cause might have had a tidy windfall - the average price for a home on the street was now £1.6 million. The affluence was understated though: there was little ostentatious about the double row of three-storey mid-Victorian terraces just north of the delicatessens and boutiques of Holland Park Avenue, and around the corner from a restaurant reportedly frequented by the likes of Gwyneth Paltrow, Naomi Campbell and Kylie Minogue. Pat Digby's house was further up from Jordan's old lair, nearer Holland Park, and on the other side of the road.

Of course, the suggestion that the knife was there, was far-fetched. Even if Digby had hidden it under the floorboards - as alleged - he surely wouldn't have left it - setting such an obvious potential trap for himself. His mother Emily had lived in the house until her death in 1968, so he would have had ample opportunity to return and remove it. But while improbable, it wasn't impossible.

The knife that killed Kelso Cochrane, according to the Home Office pathologist Dr Donald Teare, who based his analysis on the nature of the victim's wound and testing different weapons, was an ordinary stiletto-type, with a single, very sharply pointed edge. The blow was delivered with unusual power, and Teare concluded that the weapon was between five and six inches long. Assuming for a moment that it was buried somewhere in the house, what evidential value might it hold after so long?

DNA is best preserved in a cool, dry environment: conditions one might find under a floor. But there would be a host of variables. Had it been wiped clean? Had anyone else handled it? What about 'secondary transfers' - where DNA is passed from one person to another, say through a handshake, and then on to the object in question? Would there even be any trace of Kelso on it? And if so, would a DNA test on a surviving relative offer sufficient proof? Then there were the floorboards. As Frank said: *"They might have done all the houses up, modernised them and made them posh, but did they rip the floorboards up? Did they say: 'We'll just nail the floorboards down, put a bit of carpet on it.'"*

The planning records at Kensington Town Hall showed that there had been plenty of work on the property over the years. In 1996, for instance: "works of demolition in connection with [the] erection of a rear ground floor extension and formation of a roof terrace". The architect's drawing revealed nothing about the flooring, and Susie recalled the house having linoleum and tiles, and not a wooden floor at all.

But all this proved to be academic: the present owner, not

surprisingly, was unwilling to engage, leaving the question of what happened to the knife as simply rumour and conjecture - at least for now. The central accusation however, was something more. The time had come to try to talk it through.

* * *

If you wanted to live far from where anyone knew you, away from unwelcome gossip, little asides and strange looks in the street, here would be as good as anywhere. London was three hours drive away, the nearest railway station nine miles. In a quiet old market town - once famous for making the rope hangmen fastened around the necks of the condemned - it surely wouldn't be too hard to airbrush out an undesirable past.

Equally, it was the kind of place you might be enchanted by on holiday and dream of retiring to. There were quaint tea shops, old pubs with thatched roofs and low-beamed ceilings, where your afternoons could drift pleasantly by as you sat by an open fire sipping traditional ale. Just over a mile from the town was a picturesque bay and miles of craggy, unspoilt coastline, great for invigorating walks in the bracing sea air. There was no congestion, no overcrowding and little crime: the squalling seagulls were the town's major aggravation, if the local paper was to be believed. That day's front page carried a young mum's plea to holidaymakers to stop feeding the birds after they'd swooped on her four-year-old son.

"Mum Dawn said: "All of a sudden I turned round and these two seagulls from both sides came straight down just as Charlie was taking the first bit of his ice cream. It terrified him and I had to go and put him in the car."

It was in this little seaside town that Pat Digby settled sometime around 2004.

I do a double-take in the street. Is it him? An old man - tattoos, the right height, a passing resemblance to photos of Digby -

walks by hand in hand with a younger woman. We smile. I steal a glance at his tattoos. His hands are unblemished. It's not him.

The bungalow is near the end of a cul-de-sac. A smart blue car is in the drive; a budgie sits in a cage near the kitchen window. By the door is a sign warning off unsolicited callers and threatening that suspicious behaviour will be reported to the police. I ring the bell, a dog yelps, a slim woman with short grey hair appears: Pat Digby's partner.

"Is Mr Digby here?"

"No. Why?" she asks, warily.

"I'm really sorry to bother you out of the blue. I'm doing a book about Notting Hill in the 1950s…"

"Mr Digby's dead. I hope you're not digging it all up again."

"I'm sorry. How did he die, if you don't mind me asking?"

"He died of a heart attack. He died in town."

I ask if he felt pressure when the case came up again with the BBC programme about Stanley Cochrane. She thaws a little.

"I don't think so. He wasn't worried about it as such. He said: 'Yes they did take me in, but I wasn't guilty. We were all drunk.' Nobody was murdered. Well not by him anyway. I believed him fully. I had no reason not to. I'd never known him to be violent. They only took them in for questioning because they were in the locality at the same time."

I offer my condolences.

"Well it's a nice place to die I suppose. Quirky. But nice."

"Sorry to bother you."

"That's alright."

* * *

When I told Susie that the man she'd feared for so long was dead, she wasn't totally convinced. "It would be just like him to go to ground," she said, "perhaps he's living in a caravan or abroad somewhere." But Pat Digby's death certificate confirmed that he'd died of ischaemic heart disease on December 20, 2007. So if the "worst-kept secret in Notting Hill" - that he killed Kelso Cochrane - was true, then it was all over, and any lingering hope for justice was gone.

* * *

Stanley Cochrane photographed by Monty Strikes.

Friday September 3, 2010. Stanley listened without expression as Susie told her story. He'd been early, waiting for her by the ticket barrier at Leytonstone station in a white cap and smart grey jacket. She'd been up at 4am, catching the train to Euston and negotiating the madding rush hour to get there on time. Now they sat on metallic chairs at an outdoor café by the station sipping tea and coffee, the sun glancing off the silver table: the 79-year-old retired denturist and Jehovah's Witness from Antigua, and the 61-year-old grandmother from Notting Hill with a troubled past, linked by a crime that was over in an instant 51 years ago. When she'd finished, explaining too, how she'd visited Pat Digby and tried to sting a confession out of him, Stanley paused for a while, then reflected: "It was down to the police. They were the only ones who could do it."

What seemed to bother him most was that Kelso's clothes had been disposed of in 1968, thereby eliminating a possible forensic link to the killer. He then recalled, with wry a smile, the young woman detective who told him five years before that many cases like his brother's were resolved with deathbed confessions.

Susie said she was going to Kensal Green Cemetery, where Jingles, like Kelso, was buried. Did he want to come? The idea seemed to lift him.

On the tube he took a ballpoint pen and a slim black diary from his shirt pocket and started writing. *Susie Read. Patrick*

Digby. Died of a heart attack in town. Christmas 2007.

They disembarked at Notting Hill Gate and caught the number 52 bus to the cemetery. Susie was seated a row in front of him, when Stanley leaned forward and handed her a pamphlet, which promised *"All Suffering Soon to End!"*, and which had a picture of blissful couple sitting in a field of plenty on the cover. Susie flicked through it and slipped it in her pocket. As the bus rolled along Ladbroke Grove, she stared out of the window, absorbed in the landmarks of her youth: on the right, The Elgin pub, now unrecognisably chic, a little further up on the left another ancient boozer, The Kensington Park, aka the KPH, where old black and white men stood outside smoking on the pavement. Even from the outside it looked like some unholy relic.

Once inside the cemetery, Stanley discovered that Kelso's grave was blocked off behind a corrugated iron fence: the wall behind it had collapsed, and until it was fixed, an attendant explained, no-one could go near. Ignoring the instruction, the fence was yanked back, Stanley strolled across the grass, removed the branch that had fallen on the mosaic of his brother, and studied it for the first time.

Then, armed with a map and a plot number, the pair went hunting for Jingles' grave. Up and down the gravel paths: by fresh mounds with little wooden crosses, ancient Victorian tombstones overgrown with creeping vines, battered headstones jutting out of the earth at strange angles. Stanley trailed a few feet behind Susie, immersing himself in the task by crouching down and reading the plot numbers, some of which were indecipherable. But whenever they seemed to be getting close to Jingles' grave the sequence would mysteriously jump. On they vainly went: by the graves of people whose lives had spanned generations, and those who had hardly lived at all, passed Harold Pinter's resting place, and across to the far corner by the Dissenters' Chapel, once set aside for non-believers, Jews and

Muslims. After almost an hour, and with the late summer sun
bearing down, an attendant was called, who led them directly to
a black granite headstone a few feet from the waters of the Grand
Union Canal. Its inscription read:

In Loving Memory of Eugene Henry Draggon (Jingles)
Born 31.10.33
Died 4.11.93
Missed By Family And Friends
Love Always

Afterwards they sat down, and Susie told Stanley of her three
ambitions: to tell him what she knew about the murder; to
discover whether she had a sibling from Jingles - which, she
explained, she had; and to help put Pat Digby in jail.

"Well, two out of three ain't bad. And the third was virtually
impossible," he said.

Susie and her newfound half-sister had exchanged Christmas
and birthday cards, but they hadn't met. Being abandoned at
birth by her mum had fuelled a feeling of rejection that was
lodged too deep, and she was wary of embarking on a
relationship with someone whose family, she believed, never
wanted her. "I understand because of all she's been through in
her life," Susie said, "but I wish she'd give me a chance."

"Time heals all things," Stanley reassured her.

They caught the bus back down Ladbroke Grove, getting off
close to Susie's first home. Susie quickened her step as she drew
near to where Kenley Street once was. Stanley lingered,
inspecting the old Kiln on Walmer Road, where more than 150
years before the brick-makers of the Dale worked 15 hours a day
firing tiles and bricks. He peered up at the blue plaque the
Council had erected: *"This Kiln is a reminder of the 19th Century*
when potteries and brickfields were established here amid some of the
poorest conditions in London..."

Thirty yards away, Susie was on the corner of her old road. Enough traces of the past were there for her to imagine how things once were: the long gone hairdressers' on the corner, and the little sweet shop opposite where she used to buy four Blackjacks for a penny from an old Jewish lady. But her memories weren't steeped in longing. Those were unhappy days. She was glad they'd gone.

Stanley caught up and they walked the short distance to Princedale Road. Half-way down, Susie pointed up to Pat Digby's old bedroom on the first floor. Then they crossed over and entered the Prince of Wales pub, where as a girl she'd sit on the steps sipping Tizer, while Digby and her mum mingled inside. The place was filling with well-spoken, twenty-something professionals, their chatter anticipating the weekend ahead.

Susie and Stanley carried their soft drinks to the rear garden - following the route that the young Digby and his mates used to take to escape from irate taxi drivers when they would evade paying their cab fares by running into the pub and dashing out of the back on to Portland Road. Stanley sat down and closed his eyes. It had been a long day. He had walked miles. Soon he'd be back in Antigua, back knocking on doors and spreading God's word.

CHAPTER EIGHT

AFTERWORD

"It is safe to murder negroes," Vernon Johns, black Baptist minister and civil rights pioneer, Alabama, 1948.

This book has been driven by two questions: Who killed Kelso Cochrane, and why was no one caught?

If the killer's identity was common knowledge among a small, dwindling band of a certain vintage from a clutch of streets around Notting Dale, the answer to the second question was somehow more elusive.

In summary, this much can be said about the police investigation:

Within three days of the murder, the party at 18 Southam Street had become a main line of enquiry, and two young men who were there - Pat Digby and Shoggy Breagan - had been placed in the vicinity of the stabbing at around the crucial time, and were being held for questioning. Forensic samples, including clothes' fibres, were taken from them and compared to Kelso's, without any links being established.

Breagan, I've learned, had been spotted near the scene by an unnamed witness: the only positive identification amid the flurry of movement around the street corner that night. At about midnight this witness was heading up Golborne Road from the Portobello Road end. As he crossed the railway bridge, he saw two men coming towards him from the opposite direction on the same side of the street. One was running. When the police later showed him a series of photos, the witness identified this man as Breagan. He was a few feet away when Shoggy and his companion stopped and talked by the Bagwash Laundry;

Shoggy's companion had his back turned and couldn't be identified. The witness then turned right into Southam Street, where he saw George Isaacs dealing with his cab fares. He didn't see a gang of youths or Kelso lying on the pavement, and he didn't hear any shouting: the police therefore reasoned he had passed by shortly before the murder.

This identification - along with Breagan's recent release from jail for violently attacking three black men - explains why he was singled out. But why did the police focus so quickly on Digby, who had already been in custody for more than eight hours - having been held from 5pm on the Monday after the stabbing - by the time Shoggy was detained at 1.45am in the early hours of Tuesday?

When first questioned, Digby said he'd been at the Ladbroke pub that night before going on to the Southam Street party, which was about half a mile away, and claimed that he never left the party until 8am the following morning. This didn't satisfy Forbes-Leith, who - equipped with some evidence that remains hidden - continued holding him.

In a subsequent interview, Digby was somehow forced to change his story, and admitted that he had indeed left the party. He said he'd had an argument there with Breagan, and that they'd stepped outside to sort it out. By the corner of Golborne Road five youths aged around 17 or 18 had walked towards them from the direction of Kensal Road, before turning left and out of view into Southam Street. He and Breagan then turned into Southam Street and saw a black man sitting in the gutter outside the laundry: Kelso Cochrane. As they approached him, two other black men - Horatio Lewis and Ken Steele - arrived from Golborne Road. Digby and Breagan returned to the party without mentioning what they'd seen, but later told friends, and they all agreed not to tell the police "as we might quite wrongly get into trouble". Digby said he later informed Shoggy of this agreement.

When Breagan was questioned, his story matched Digby's in its basic elements. He said he'd arrived at the party at about 11.15pm after drinking at the Earl of Warwick, and saw many people he knew, including Digby. After about 45 minutes he and Digby left Ma O'Brien's. Here their stories diverged: rather than stepping outside to fight each other, Shoggy said they went looking for girls. An inconsistency, like Digby's earlier denial of never having left the party at all, that didn't satisfy the police, who decided to hold him "pending corroboration".

When I interviewed him almost fifty years on, Shoggy Breagan revealed something remarkable about what happened next. After being questioned, he said he was taken to the cells.

"Patsy was there. Patsy was in the next cell. I shouted out, 'Patsy what did you tell the police?' He said, 'I told them we were going to have a fight.'" And when Shoggy was questioned again, that's exactly what he said. Their stories now tallying, the police released them, as there were "no grounds to continue the detention".

"They [the police] said: 'Why didn't you say that in the first place?" said Shoggy all those years later. *"You've caused a lot of trouble'."*

The weight a prosecutor could have placed on this discrepancy is open to question. Yet apparently ignorant that the two young men had been able to straighten their stories, Forbes-Leith's conclusion was that: "Whatever theory is put forward, one must not lose sight of the fact that a group of youths were involved. This group has not been identified and no information has come forward to suggest who they might be. Whether Breagan and Digby were part of it, joined in at the time or later or indeed were not in any way responsible, is not known."

Putting Digby and Breagan in next door cells was a glaring error, but not the only one.

Joy Okine's mother - who witnessed the attack with her daughter through the window of their first-floor flat on Golborne Road - was quoted in two newspapers (the *Daily Telegraph* and the

News Chronicle) saying that she saw one of the assailants try to grab an iron railing to use as a weapon. Yet the police never followed this up. A decorated former officer who was policing in the district in 1959, and who studied the available evidence in this case, maintains: "A serious opportunity was missed there. Chances are that anyone who was prepared to use the railing as a weapon already had his dabs [fingerprints] on file as well as the fence."

At least two further aspects of the investigation warrant closer examination.

First, the hunt for the murder weapon. To a fanfare of publicity, the police searched for the knife in 30 drains around the murder spot and swept the bottom of the Grand Union Canal with a giant magnet. But was the obvious step ever taken of searching the suspects' homes, and in particular Pat Digby's? I have found no evidence it was.

Second, the disposal of Kelso's clothes, which so perturbed Stanley Cochrane. They were tested for blood and fibres after the murder, and nine years later were destroyed, with the "proper authority" say the police. The rules regarding retaining evidence were different in 1968 to today, and even if the clothes had been kept, their potential value would depend on certain conditions: they would need to have been kept in a sterile environment at an optimum temperature, for example, and to have not deteriorated or been mishandled. According to the experts I spoke to, advances in forensic science mean that, although unlikely, there was nevertheless still a possibility that the brown jacket, blue trousers and open-necked grey and black striped shirt that Kelso wore the night he was killed, could have provided a link to his assailants years later.

Beyond these specifics, there's a broader point to consider. While the investigation was unfolding against the backdrop of the *Sunday Express* leak inquiry and threats to the careers of the detectives suspected of passing information to the paper, it was also happening amid fears that Kelso's death might trigger a reprisal - or worse - of the previous summer's race riot.

Evidence of the authorities' anxieties and their desire to not only calm tensions, but to see the case recede from public view, is overwhelming. The Prime Minister Harold Macmillan convened a special meeting of ministers to discuss the murder and the situation in Notting Hill. The Home Secretary was kept abreast of developments with regular briefings. As the Union Movement descended on the district for Mosley's election campaign, and left-wing groups discussed setting up defence committees "to sweep the fascists off the streets", Special Branch kept a beady eye. Extra police were ordered in and detectives ruled out any racial motive in the killing. Meanwhile, behind the scenes, civil servants and West Indian politicians deliberated about "discrediting" the activists unifying around Kelso's death, and of repatriating his body so that his grave wouldn't become a site for "annual pilgrimages" by "mischief-makers" - though only after "a reasonable interval" to avoid "undue publicity". When no-one was charged after three months, the Colonial Office cautioned the West Indian authorities against going public with their concerns. And, on August 27, 1959, when Garnet Gordon, the Commissioner for the West Indies, rang Sir Joseph Simpson, the Met Police Commissioner, to ask about the case's progress, Simpson suggested that *"we had got as far as we could and were balked from taking any further action due to lack of evidence which was unlikely ever to be made good"* - a peculiarly pessimistic stance, coming just twelve weeks after a murder in which many undoubtedly knew the perpetrator.

From here - and moving into the realm of speculation - is it going too far to imagine that the will to convict just wasn't there, that it was considered best to *let it lie*?

After all, if the four-year jail terms handed down by Justice Salmon to the nine white youths for their "nigger-hunting" expedition stirred such resentment and was seized upon as a gross miscarriage of justice in some quarters, what might have been unleashed by a young white man going to the gallows for murdering a black man?

A foretaste came just eight days before Kelso's death, when Ron Marwood, a 25-year-old scaffolder from Islington, was hanged for stabbing policeman Ray Summers in the back and leaving him bleeding to death on the pavement, after the young PC tried to break up a fight outside a dance hall on the Seven Sisters Road, north London. Marwood's execution, on May 8 1959, was met with a wave of protest: more than 150 MPs appealed for a reprieve, around 1,000 people - ghouls as well as anti-death penalty protestors - gathered by Pentonville prison on the morning he was killed, and a gang of Teddy Boys later charged Tower Hill police station, chanting "Revenge for Marwood" and "All coppers are bastards". With its racial and political overtones, a far deadlier storm would have brewed in Kelso's case.

Yet without hard proof that a cold calculation was made somewhere down the line - in other words, that justice was subverted in the name of the greater public good, and that the murderer allowed to slip through the net - it's also possible to make the opposite case. That the authorities would have been aware that a failure to convict anyone would poison the already damaged relations between black people and the police, and that Kelso's death would become a totem to the idea that black and white were treated differently by the law. The evidence, however, doesn't indicate that the authorities were especially preoccupied by this concern.

Finally, we must examine the police's attitude to the victim.

Hard-working, ambitious, and still spoken of fondly and with genuine emotion by those who knew him, Kelso was briefly elevated into an icon through his death; his name signifying all the racial struggles and injustice of the time. Yet in life he was no paragon. He was deported from America when it was discovered that his visa had expired, after he'd been charged with assault on his wife Kansas Green in June 1953. She received "lacerations to her forearms", though later withdrew the charges and supported his application for US citizenship when he was in London. When the police learned of his history, the press were tipped off, just as they had been about his murder.

On May 24 1959, *The People* newspaper ran a front page story headlined *Gang Victim Led Double Life:*

"A new theory about the death of 32-year-old Kelso Cochrane, the coloured carpenter stabbed in Notting Hill a week ago, emerged last night from a detailed investigation of Cochrane's background. The facts are that Cochrane had been drinking on the night of his death and was known to be truculent after a few drinks. He had a conviction for causing grievous bodily harm to a workmate, whom he attacked with a spanner. The knife that killed him was probably his own. He liked to carry one. And police think he may have lied to his friends about his wrist injury, which he said was caused at work. They believe 6ft 2in Cochrane was more likely to have broken his wrist in a fight he preferred not to talk about. The fight, indeed, may have had something to do with his death. Cochrane fled to his 'fiancée', a coloured nurse, when he said he was a bachelor. He has a wife and family in America. Yard men believe he was carrying the knife when he ran into a gang of youths on the corner of Southam Street and Goldborne [sic] Road, North Kensington in the early hours of Whit Sunday. The theory is that the youths demanded the money. Cochrane drew his knife and one of the youths, in the struggle, forced the knife into his chest. Police are still searching for the knife. Cochrane's 'fiancée' 21-year-old nurse Olivia Ellington, said last night: 'Kelso married? This is a shock. We were to marry in June.'"

The article, even allowing for possible embellishments by the paper, was directly sourced to the police, and riddled with falsehoods. Olivia Ellington had already told the police that she had "never seen him the worse for drinking" and that "he always drank in moderation", while Dr Teare's post-mortem found no trace of alcohol in Kelso's body. His workmates confirmed to the police that the accident at work was just that and nothing more (he was also described as "an exceptionally good worker" and "well thought of" by his employer). And the idea that Kelso, his left hand in plaster, pulled a knife on the youths after they demanded money, and then had it wrestled off him before being stabbed in the heart, all in the few, brief moments in which the attack occurred, and that no witnesses saw anything of the kind, was faintly ridiculous. Yet by planting this suggestion in the media, and by drawing attention to Kelso's past, someone within the force was implying that an innocent black man killed while walking down the road minding his own business, somehow deserved his fate.

Add it together - the leaks, the placing of the two suspects in adjacent cells, no fingerprints taken from the iron railings - and the conclusion is plain. Even allowing for the wisdom of hindsight, and acknowledging the real challenge of investigating a crime in which people were reluctant to speak and threats were flying, Kelso Cochrane had little chance of ever getting justice.

Ghosts of Notting Hill

As well as an unsolved murder, this book is about an area and its people.

Today swathes of Notting Hill have become an exotic playground for millionaires, a haunt of bankers, media folk, celebrities, and the Tory party's elite; a place known across the world for Richard Curtis's twee romantic blockbuster, and the biggest street carnival in Europe, which was founded in a spirit of resistance from the embers of the 1958 riots. It's where the wealthy middle-classes have moved en masse, drawn by a vibrant street life and the district's cosmopolitan edginess. Yet the more they settle there, the more that vitality disappears.

Another Notting Hill, one that's less known or talked about, is that of its old white working-class. It may seem out of kilter with this book's subject matter, but it's important to state: the culture and history of the people whose roots in the district run so deep, is worth celebrating. However virulent the racism that fuelled the riots and Kelso's murder, however few came forward to identify the culprits, and however deeply some felt that black and white mixing was an abomination, this is only part of the story, and certainly not its end.

For one thing, Notting Dale was never an island of bigotry in a sea of tolerance. From the slave trade to the Empire, racism was sewn into the fabric of British society. Colin Prescod, a Ladbroke Grove film-maker and sociologist, arrived in the area as a child from Trinidad just before the riots, and saw his mother campaign against discrimination with Claudia Jones. "The greatness of Britain was built on ideologies of superiority," he argues. "To think that Britain's history is one of only white working-class racism towards black people is a nonsense. It was institutionalised by the ruling class."

What's more, it was the people in the Dale's wretched slums, not those in the secluded mansions with manicured gardens on Holland Park's summit, for instance, who saw their neighbourhood change through mass immigration. And even when the enmity and violence were at their peak, many in Notting Dale were happy to live, work and start families with their new neighbours. Hordes turned out for Kelso's funeral, and Mosley was humiliated in the 1959 General Election. In the end, despite the convulsions, people by and large adapted, and hybrid cultures have emerged. Many of the black and white grandchildren of people who fought each other in the riots now speak in the same multi-ethnic London dialect, listen to the same music, and wear their jeans in the same style (halfway down their backsides).

But change, always inevitable, comes in different forms. Another, just as striking, has been to Notting Hill itself. Traditional boozers have been replaced by gastro pubs, and working men's cafes supplanted by fashionable delis. Spiralling rents have driven out small retailers, and corporate chains have moved in. Meanwhile the council is lining up old estates for demolition in the name of redevelopment and unlocking the value of the land. The upshot is that the place in Notting Hill for its oldest tribe seems to shrink by the day.

NOTES AND SOURCES

Prologue

1) Phone call to the *Sunday Express* news desk after midnight and Frank Draper's unlikely 'recollection' of it: MEPO 2/9883

2) Whitsun Bank Holiday traffic and weather reports: the *Star*, May 16, 1959, *Jams and Crashes Mount*; *News of the World*, May 17, 1959, *It's a Bumper (To Bumper) Whitsun*; *The People*, May 17, 1959, *Don't Come Home Tonight*.

3) 11 Bevington Road 1959 description: Interview with George Birch, resident and Kelso Cochrane's neighbour. September, 2009.

4) The details of Kelso's last day and his route to the hospital are drawn from Olivia Ellington's statement to the coroner Gavin Thurston, August 1959; her police statement, May 1959; and a confidential source.

5) The spate of disturbances around the route of Kelso's journey come from MEPO 2/9883; *Manchester Guardian*, May 18, 1959, *More Violence in North Kensington*.

6) Kelso's treatment at Paddington General Hospital is based on Dr John Givans' statement to the coroner Gavin Thurston, August 1959; as well as interviews with Dr Givans, December 2005.

7) Details of the attack: Coroner's report, August 1959; confidential source.

8) Arthur Cook article, *Daily Mail*, May 18, 1959. *At Race Murder Corner*.

9) Telegram from Whitehall to the West Indies: CO 1031/2541. Other correspondence that underlines the authorities' anxiety that the murder might lead to more trouble, includes a confidential telegram from Lord Hailes, Governor General of the West Indies Federation, to Lord

Perth, Secretary of State for the Colonies, on 19, May, 1959, which reads: *"Prime Minister [of the West Indies Federation, Sir Grantley Adams] has received telegram from Commissioner [of the West Indies in the UK] referring to the murder of Kelso Cochrane in North Kensington last Sunday. Commissioner concludes: 'Careful investigations disclose very unsettled situation. Letter follows.' Can you tell me very urgently what is your assessment of this incident? Do you anticipate further developments?"* Source: CO 131/2541

10) Newspaper descriptions of Kelso as a quiet man who liked jazz, see for example: *Daily Express*, May 18, 1959; *Daily Mirror*, May 19, 1959.

11) Committee of African Organisations' emergency meeting and letter to Harold Macmillan, are based, among other sources, on *The Daily Worker*, May 20, 1959, *Mass Funeral March Plan*.

12) Despite the perpetrators reportedly confessing to FBI agents, no-one was ever convicted for Mack Charles Parker's murder.

13) *"...We shall have given the green light to every 'nigger-baiting' Teddy Boy in Notting Hill"*: Barbara Castle quoted in the *Daily Telegraph*, May 19 1959.

14) Special Branch's observation that *"The murder of the West Indian attracted considerable public attention in the West Indies"*: HO 344/34

15) Inter-Racial Friendship Co-ordinating Council members visit the Home Office: HO 344/34; *The Daily Worker*, May 28, 1959. *Stop Race Hate Move.*

A Special Branch report from this time describes Claudia Jones as: *"a well-known West Indian communist who came to this country in 1955 rather than await deportation proceedings against her, because of communist activities in the United States of America."* On July 1, 1959 Special Branch monitored the Council's meeting at the Friends' Centre, Tavistock Square,

WC1. According to the officer, ten people attended and Amy Ashwood Garvey was elected chairman and Claudia Jones vice-chair. *"It was agreed future activities of the council should include 1) Campaigning for the apprehension of the murderer of Kelso Cochrane 2) Campaigning for a law against the incitement of racial hatred and racial discrimination."* See: HO 325/9

16) 'We Mourn Cochrane' public meeting: HO 344/34; British Pathé archive news footage; *The Times*, May 28 1959; *News Chronicle*, May 29 1959. Three weeks after the Cochrane memorial meeting Huddleston co-founded the anti-apartheid movement.

17) Radio Moscow broadcast: *News Chronicle*, May 29 1959.

18) Whitehall demonstration: British Pathé archive footage, *Kensington Post*, June 5 1959, *Colour protest in Whitehall*.

19) Rab Butler statement on the murder in the House of Commons: *Hansard*, June 4, 1959; *Daily Herald*, June 5, 1959, *Police May Get Coloured Recruits Soon; Daily Express*, June 5, 1959, *Rab Makes History With Murder Plea*.

20) Rab Butler raises the prospect of recruiting black policemen. This was discussed at a Home Office meeting about the Cochrane case and the situation in Notting Hill attended by Met Police Commissioner Sir Joseph Simpson on June 2, 1959. The Home Secretary and Ministers for Health, Housing and Education were present. Simpson noted that Notting Hill was *"traditionally disorderly and the concentration of colonial immigrants had aggravated the problem"*. He also argued that *"it was not desirable to recruit coloured policemen"*. According to a note of the meeting, the prospect of setting up of an independent inquiry *"to examine the problems of the areas which had received large numbers of coloured immigrants"* was also raised, but rejected because it *"might make recommendations unacceptable to the government"*. Source: HO 325/9. It was eight years before the Met Police accepted its first black policeman. Norwell Roberts joined the force on March

27 1967 - an event which was marked by his appearance on the cover of *Private Eye*. After a distinguished 30-year career, Roberts was awarded a Queen's Police Medal in 1996.

21) Funeral scene sources: *Kensington News*: June 12, 1959, *1,200 Mourn Cochrane*; *The Times*, June 8, *Big Crowd at West Indian's Funeral*, *The Daily Worker*, June 8 1959; *The Observer*, June 7, 1959, *700 Mourn Murdered West Indian*; British Pathé Archive news footage.

22) Special Branch report on the funeral and reference to the questioning of Sherriff Sesay: HO 344/34.

23) March in honour of Kelso, June 7, 1959 and Sesay's proposal to erect a statue in Antigua, *Daily Mirror*, June 8, 1959 and HO 344/34.

24) Reward for information leading to the conviction of the killer, *News of the World*, June 7, 1959, *Our £2,500 Reward – Find the Notting Hill Killers.*

25) Stanley Cochrane's recollections and approach to Scotland Yard to re-open the investigation into his brother's murder, interviews: December 2005 - September 2010.

26) Details of Kelso's moves to Dominica and the United States and his subsequent deportation back to Antigua: CO 131/2541. Kelso's daughter Josephine still lives in New York and is a Muslim convert.

27) Kelso's departure for England on the French liner, Colombie: National Archives, immigrant passenger lists, September 1954.

Chapter One: One Foot in the Grove

28) *"We gain our knowledge of life in catastrophic form..."* Bertolt Brecht's quote is from an article he wrote on detective stories, cited in *Delightful Murder: A Social History of the Crime*, Ernest Mandel, 1984.

29) For the purposes of this book, Notting Hill describes the

area encompassing most of W10 and W11. Though it has no official boundaries, many define Notting Hill as being located within a tighter radius of the tube station.

30) WH Wills, assistant editor of Dickens' *Household Words* magazine penned the article on the Potteries (as Notting Dale was known then), in the first edition of the magazine in March 1850. The reference to conditions surpassing even those in Ireland was perhaps stretching things, as local historian Tom Vague has noted.

31) *"The inhabitants all look unhealthy..."* is from an official report referred to in *Notting Hill and Holland Park Past*, Barbara Denny, Historical Publications, 1993.

32) For more detail on mortality rates in Notting Dale during this period see also, *Survey of London, Volume XXXVIII, North Kensington*, The Athlone Press, University of London, 1973. *"During the years 1846-48 living conditions at The Potteries had become so appalling that the average age at the time of death among the 1,056 inhabitants was only 11 years and seven months, compared with an average at death throughout the whole of London of 37 years."*

33) Locals seeking oblivion in alcohol and the number of pubs in the Dale, see: *Notting Hill in bygone days,* Florence Gladstone and Ashley Barker, Anne Bingley Publisher, 1923 and 1969.

34) Colin MacInnes' quote is from *The Observer*, January 21, 1962, *Poverty and Poetry in W10*.

35) Campaign to change the Portobello's name. *Kensington Post*, January 9 1959, *Withdraw call to Portobello rebels*.

36) Reminisces of life in Notting Dale in the 1950s is also based on interviews with various old residents.

37) Evidence of Sir Walter Raleigh's kinship with 'Charles', a young Guyanese boy whom he apparently brought to England from the Americas, can be found in the baptism register in the London Metropolitan Archives. See also: *The*

Times, January 24, 2009. *Sir Walter Raleigh May Have Adopted Native Boy From Guyana.*

38) Frederick Pease's death is recorded in Kensington Library's local history section in a certificate describing him as a "film actor" aged 60, whose identification marks were "negro", and who died as a result of a "bomb blast" on 19.2.41.

39) Four and five-storey Victorian houses built in the Colville area in the 1860s, see: *Beyond the Mother Country,* Ed Pilkington, IB Tauris and Co, Ltd, 1988.

40) Descriptions of keeping the milk in the sink, cooking scrags on the landing et al, are based on interviews with various West Indian migrants to Notting Hill.

41) Interview with the late Roy Stewart, 2005. RIP. 15.6.25 – 27.10.08.

42) References to the Apollo pub on All Saints Road, Sarah Churchill visiting Totobags and the Rio, see: *Beyond the Mother Country,* Ed Pilkington, IB Tauris and Co, Ltd, 1988; *Windrush: The Irresistible Rise of Multi-Racial Britain,* Mike Phillips and Trevor Phillips, HarperCollins, reissue 2009; *Notting Hill in the Sixties:* Charlie Phillips and Mike Phillips, Lawrence & Wishart, 1991.

43) The Gathering Storm in Ladbroke Grove: *Kensington News,* August 15, 1958, *Violence Wave.*

44) Details of the August 24, 1958 attacks on MacDonald Waldron, Matthew Lucien, John Pirmal, Joseph Welsh and James Ettiene, as well as the statements of the nine youths responsible are contained in CRIM 1/3030.

45) The appearance of the nine youths at West London Magistrate's Court is from the *Kensington Post,* September 1 and 5 1958; *Beyond the Mother Country,* Ed Pilkington, IB Tauris and Co, Ltd, 1988; ER Guest description courtesy of former police constable who spent many an hour in West London Magistrates' Court.

46) Weather description for the evening of August 29, 1958: the

National Meteorological Archive.

47) Majbritt Morrison charted her journey from housewife to prostitute in her autobiography, *Jungle West 11*, published by Tandem. It concludes, at the age of 30, with her escaping her life on the streets after a jail term "for dope" and a bout of alcoholism. There was a legal distinction between a pimp and a ponce at the time: a ponce battened on to prostitutes, a pimp importuned clients for them.

48) Descriptions of the mob in Bramley Road and Majbritt Morrison's arrest are from *Jungle West 11*, Majbritt Morrison, Tandem, and *Manchester Guardian*, September 2, 1958.

49) The late King Dick's account of the attack on his Blechynden Street blues' party is based on his interview in *Windrush: The Irresistible Rise of Multi-Racial Britain*, Mike Phillips and Trevor Phillips, HarperCollins, reissue 2009.

50) Perhaps the most vivid reporting of the riots was Colin Eales' in the *Kensington News*. For instance: *Witness to Violence*, September 5 1958: *"They came on foot, by train, bus, motor bike, car and lorry, shouting 'Alright boys we're here,'"* Eales wrote. In Talbot Grove, he spoke to a group of cheerful housewives and their husbands. *"I was told that they were expecting a gang of negroes led by a female brothel-keeper to come down and set on them. As we chatted amicably on the door-step a woman shouted: 'Here comes Madame! Men and women alike pulled out railings and iron bars. Some grabbed milk bottles. A solitary coloured man ran down the street being pelted with bottles. When the excitement had subsided one woman breathed a sigh of relief and said: 'Wrong ones'."*

51) For reports of black and white children playing together during the riots, see *The Times*, September 3, 1958. In one of the streets where some of the worst fighting had occurred, *The Times'* man *"found a group of men in a public house singing 'Ol' Man River' and 'Bye Bye Blackbird' and punctuating the songs with vicious anti-Negro slogans. The men said that their*

motto was Keep Britain White and they made all sorts of wild charges against their coloured neighbours...There are three main causes of resentment against coloured inhabitants of the district. They are alleged to do no work and to collect a rich sum from the Assistance Board. They are said to be able to find housing when white residents cannot. And they are charged with all kinds of misbehaviour, especially sexual..."

52) Details of the West Indian fight-back staged from Totobag's come from the *Daily Mail*, September 2, 1958. *37 Arrested as the Siege of Blenheim Crescent brings London's third night of battle.* See also: *Kensington News*, September 5 1958, *Witness to Violence; Beyond the Mother Country*, Ed Pilkington, *Daily Mail* September 2, 1958. The following year, 9 Blenheim Crescent became home to the Africa Asia League, one of the many civil rights' groups that sprung up in the wake of Kelso's murder and the riots.

53) The rain falls and the riots end, September 3, 1958. Sources: Ruth Glass, *London's Newcomers, The West Indian Migrants*, Harvard University Press, 1960; *Manchester Guardian*, September 4, 1958. *Empty Streets and Rain*. Around sixty per cent of those arrested in the riots were under 20 years of age according to Glass.

54) Ed Pilkington's *Beyond the Mother Country*, IB Tauris and Co, Ltd, 1988, provides an in-depth account of the 1958 Nottingham disturbances, as well as those in Notting Hill.

55) The *Manchester Guardian's* report on the Cardiff riots relied on a "prominent Cardiff citizen who takes a leading part in social work" for its wider context. He said: *"The black man is not alone to blame, and the problem of his association with white girls must be tackled, however, it should always be kept in mind that the type of black man now in the port is quite different from the pre-war negro. He is not so well acquainted with British customs, has the ways of thought of his native villages, and is fresh for trouble."* *Manchester Guardian*, June 12, 1919, *Serious*

Racial Riots at Cardiff.

56) Liverpool Riots. *New York Times*, June 13, 1919, *Race Riots Break Out in British Cities.*

57) Jamaica's Chief Minister Norman Manley's 'Little Rock' quote: *Manchester Guardian*, September 4, 1958.

58) *New York Herald Tribune* columnist identifies communists behind the riots, see: Ruth Glass, *London's Newcomers, The West Indian Migrants*, Harvard University Press, 1960.

59) *Die Burger* newspaper reference, see *Manchester Guardian*, August 28, 1958. The paper was referring specifically to Nottingham's riots.

60) *"A comprehensive Immigration Bill is being urgently studied by officials..."* DO 35/7990. The Commonwealth Immigrants Act of 1962 was the end result: it placed new controls on Commonwealth passport holders, requiring prospective immigrants to apply for a work voucher which was graded according to the applicant's employment prospects.

61) The South African writer Dan Jacobson attended the nine youth's trial and wrote a perceptive essay entitled *After Notting Hill* for *Encounter* magazine, December 1958, volume XI, number 6. He concluded: *"[The nine youths] and a great many of those who followed their example - felt themselves in some special and terrible way permitted to attack the coloureds who were their victims; and that in their attitudes to what they did (and their parents to them and the court) there was an element of something approaching self-righteousness, which could have been absent had their victims belonged to some other group, or gang."*

62) Mr Justice Salmon's speech and the sentencing of the nine youths, see: *Manchester Guardian*, September 16, 1958, *Nine Youths Sent to Prison for Four Years*; *Shepherd's Bush Gazette*, September 19, 1958; *Daily Mail*, September 16, 1958, *Nine 'nigger hunters' get 4 years*; *Daily Mirror*, September 16, 1958, *Four Years' Prison For Nine White Thugs*. Salmon was the first Jewish judge to sit on the Queen's Bench Division since Lord

Reading more than 30 years before - a fact noted by many Mosleyites. Description of the scene outside the Old Bailey and a man shouting: *"Four years! My boy's life is ruined..."* is from Dan Jacobson's *Encounter* article.

63) Support for the nine young men wasn't confined to the run-down quarters of Notting Dale and White City. Those arguing for leniency included Fenner Brockway, a left-wing Labour MP and staunch campaigner for laws against racial discrimination. Brockway pleaded with Home Secretary Rab Butler for the four year sentences to be reduced by Royal Prerogative. *"These youths are only 17, 18 and 19. Admittedly they ran riot, but in my view they are as much the victims of the hysteria that swept over Notting Hill as the West Indians,"* he declared. Butler was unmoved, telling the House of Commons: *"I know of no grounds which would justify me in recommending the exercise of the Royal Prerogative of mercy in these cases."* Sources: *The Times*, September 26 1958 and August 19 1959; *Hansard*, December 11 1958.

"Some of the finest faces you could wish to see..."

64) Jeffrey Hamm's rabble-rousing at Oxford Gardens School. See: *Shepherd's Bush Gazette*, March 13, 1959. *These lads are no thugs, says Mosley man.* One boy's father had a letter published in the UM's *North Kensington Leader*. *"I have no colour prejudice nor racial antagonism,"* he wrote, *"but where am I after a lifetime of two wars and mass unemployment! Nine youths two years from school, are put away for 36 years to make my country safe for strangers."* According to another parent, 10,000 people signed the petition to reduce the youth's sentences, *Daily Mirror*, November 26, 1958; *Kensington News*, November 28, 1958.

65) *"They tried to make Notting Hill a bad word..."* *North Kensington Leader*, Number 9, July / August 1959.

66) The *Daily Mail* described Oswald Mosley as the *"paramount*

political personality in Britain" and claimed that his British Union of Fascists party was *"caught up on such a wave of deep-seated popular enthusiasm as must sweep it to victory"*. The paper said that Britain's survival depended on *"the existence of a Great Party of the Right with the same directness of purpose and energy of method as Hitler and Mussolini have displayed."* See: Stephen Dorril, *Black Shirt: Sir Oswald Mosley and British Fascism*, Penguin Global, 2008.

67) Weather description October 7, 1958: National Meteorological Archive.

68) Mosley's meeting at the Earl of Warwick, see: *Kensington News*, October 10 1958; *"his eyes dilating hypnotically in trademark fashion..."*: see BBC archive footage. The comparison of Mosley to Douglas Fairbanks senior and description of him as a *"soldierly figure remarkably untouched by the years"*, *Kensington News*, November 14, 1958, *Some of these 'Teds' are Fine Fellows*.

69) Details of Oswald Mosley's meeting at Argyll Hall, Lancaster Road, W11, April 6, 1959: HO 344/34; *The Times*, April 7 1959, *Sir O Mosley on the Colour Problem*.

70) *"We should get hold of an immigrant and hang him upside-down from Blackfriar's Bridge..."* This incident is cited in Trevor Grundy's *Memoir of a Fascist Childhood, A Boy in Mosley's Britain*, Heinemann, 1998. The UM member who made the comment is named as Peter Shaw - a pseudonym says Grundy.

71) Colin Jordan and the White Defence League. For Special Branch reports on Jordan and the WDL, see: HO 344/34; for *Black and White News*, see: HO 325/9. Residents' complaints about activities at the White Defence League's Princedale Road HQ, *Kensington News*, August 24, 1962. For Dr Arnold Leese's history, see: Stephen Dorril, *Black Shirt: Sir Oswald Mosley and British Fascism*, Penguin Global, 2008. The quote, *"Notting Hill, remember, is still part of England..."* is from an

interview with Colin Jordan, *Daily Herald*, June 15, 1959. *Hate Peddlers!* See also: *Daily Herald*, June 12, 1959, *Ban This Race Hate Leaflet.*

Chapter Two: White Men like You

72) Kelso's other addresses in England included: 14 Oakington Road, W14; 9 Acklam Road, W10; 21 Bevington Road, W10 (where he lived with his two unmarried sisters); and 14 Oakington Road, W9.

73) Kelso's application for US citizenship is accepted; his wife meets another man; he meets Olivia Ellington: all from a confidential source.

74) Friends' descriptions of Kelso: interview with Rose Christian, June 17, 2009, and with Samuel Fayne, December 2005.

75) Rose Christian cooks for Kelso and he visits the Christians three days before his death: interview with Rose Christian, June 17, 2009.

76) Eyewitness accounts of the murder from Horatio Lewis and Kenneth Steele are drawn from: their statements to the coroner Gavin Thurston, August 1959; interview with Horatio Lewis, January 2006; confidential source.

77) Joy Okine and her mother witness the murder: *Daily Telegraph*, May 18 1959; *News Chronicle*, May 18, 1959.

78) George Isaacs sees the scuffle on the corner of Southam Street: his statement to the coroner, Gavin Thurston, August, 1959; and confidential source.

79) *"They asked me for money..."* is from Kenneth Steele's statement to coroner, Gavin Thurston, August, 1959.

80) Kelso is taken to St Charles' Hospital and seen by Dr Mohammed Seddiq; Detective Sergeant Sidney Coomber arrives at the hospital; Coomber informs Steele and Lewis of his death: MEPO 2/9883.

81) Dr Donald Teare's post-mortem details are in the coroner's

report into Kelso Cochrane's death.

The Pride of Hendon

82) Ian Forbes-Leith's background: interview with former police colleague of his, December 2005; interview with F-L's relative Pamela Moffatt, December 2010; his police career details are also from MEPO 21/03. Further biographical details: *Paddington Mercury*, May 8, 1959.

83) Forbes-Leith joins the police under the Trenchard scheme, see: *Bent Coppers*, James Morton, Time Warner paperbacks 2002. Lord Trenchard, Metropolitan Police Commissioner from 1931-35, introduced the scheme to attract 'officer material' to the force. Ambitious young high-fliers like Forbes-Leith, it was thought, wouldn't plod the pavements for 10 years, and so were offered the chance of accelerated promotion through the newly-created rank of junior Station Inspector after a two-year course at Hendon. The Labour MP Aneurin Bevin derided the Trenchard scheme as: *"an entirely fascist development, designed to make the police force more amenable to the orders of the Carlton Club and Downing Street."*

84) Forbes-Leith's meteoric rise through the ranks: *Daily Telegraph*, February 27, 1961, *Police Chief to Resign*.

85) Dorothy Lewis / Napoleon Ryder case, see: *Manchester Guardian*, July 2 1954, *Widow in Wills Case Gaoled, Seven Years for Friend*.

86) Bernard Smeeth breaks into the manse and assaults Mrs Edith Spivey, see: *Daily Express*, September, 12 1956, *Five Years for Night Raid at the Manse*.

87) Brighton corruption case, see: *Manchester Guardian*, March 1 1958, *Brighton Detectives had no 'Moral Leadership'*; Forbes-Leith is called *'the Pride of Hendon'*, see: *Daily Express*, February 28, 1958.

88) Forbes-Leith takes up his new post at Harrow Road:

Paddington Mercury, May 8, 1959, *Yard Man is new CID Chief.*

89) Details of the first steps in the police investigation are from MEPO 2/9883.

90) The police call on James and Rose Christian early on Sunday morning with news of Kelso's death: interview with Rose Christian, June 17, 2009; also *Windrush: The Irresistible Rise of Multi-Racial Britain*, Mike Phillips and Trevor Phillips, HarperCollins, reissue 2009.

91) Olivia Ellington visits the Christians before work and her newspaper quotes are from: *Daily Express*, May 18, 1959, *The Dusky Girl in a Notting Hill Room* by George Gale; and *Daily Herald*, May 18, 1959.

92) People gather at the Christians' home and drink to Kelso's memory; James Christian doesn't stop crying: interview with Samuel Fayne, a friend of Kelso's present that day, December 2005.

93) Extra police sweep into Notting Hill and Rab Butler is kept updated on the situation: *Daily Telegraph* May 19 1959, *Mr Butler Told of Murder Hunt*; *Evening Standard*, May 18, 1959.

94) The Bank Holiday Fair at Wormwood Scrubs and the incident with the dodgems: *The Times*, May 19, 1959. See also: *Star*, May 18, 1959, *Killer Hunt Swoop on Fairs*. Weather description for the day: National Meteorological Archive.

95) *"The stabbing has absolutely nothing to do with racial conflict. The motive could have been robbery"*: *The Times*, May 19, 1959, *Race Tension increased by Murder*. *Daily Mirror* quotes: May 19, 1959, *The Yard and the Notting Hill Murder*.

96) *"...One or more of the teenage gang could face a charge of murder in the furtherance of robbery. The penalty for this is HANGING."* Under the 1957 Homicide Act this was one of the categories of murder for which the death penalty remained - along with murder by firearms or explosion; killing in resisting arrest or escaping from custody; and killing a police or

prison officer on duty.

97) Allan Morais, Deputy Commissioner for the West Indies, says the notion that the murder wasn't racist is *"complete and utter nonsense"*, see: *News Chronicle*, May 19, 1959, *Envoy Clashes with Yard in Murder Hunt*. Bob Pennington, of the Socialist Labour League, later wrote: *"Every coloured person I spoke to in the area endorses Morais's statement...In the Earl of Warwick, a public house twenty yards from the scene of the murder, a coloured railway worker angrily retorted, 'The police are talking rubbish, man. Everyone knows thieves don't hunt in packs of six.'"*

98) Sir Oswald Mosley issued a statement about the murder on Tuesday May 19, 1959. See: *Kensington Post*, May 22, 1959, *Mosley Speaks*.

99) Ian Forbes-Leith splits his men into three teams: *Evening Standard*, May 21, 1959, *Murder Hunt Knife in Drains*.

100) The 1951 census found that 12.7% of the population in Golborne Ward lived at a density of more than two persons per room. For London as a whole the average was 2.5%. Descriptions of Southam Street are based on various photographs, residents' memories, and Ruth Glass's depiction in *London's Newcomers, The West Indian Migrants*, Harvard University Press, 1961.

101) Ma O'Brien's *"good as gold"* quote: *Daily Express*, May 19 1959.

102) Seven youths abuse a passing black stranger after leaving a wedding party on Golborne Road: confidential source.

103) Police search North Kensington's grimy nooks and corners for the knife: *The Times*, May 22, 1959, *Search for Weapon in North Kensington*; *Evening Standard*, May 21, 1959, *Murder Hunt Knife in Drains*; *Star*, May 22, 1959; *News Chronicle*, May 23 1959.

104) Kelso had no known enemies in the district: confidential source.

The Notting Hill Squad

105) Locals youths 'try to find the murderer': *Daily Express*, May 20, 1959 *The posse in tight trousers hunts a killer.* The same story - *"of unexpected help for the police"* from local boys named as Brian Donaghue, Peter and Mark Bell and George Baker - was also covered in the *Kensington Post*, May 22, 1959, *Search For A Knife And A Killer.*

106) Breagan and Digby quotes and descriptions of scenes following their release from Harrow Road station: *Daily Herald*, May 21, 1959, *My 44 Hour Ordeal in Murder Quiz; Daily Mirror*, May 21, 1959, *Man who helped Notting Hill murder probe tells of – My 45 hrs with the Police; Daily Express*, May 21, 1959, *Youths go home after 50 hours, Shoggy - 'I thought I would end up being topped', Digby -'We decided to get out of it fast.'*

107) On December 14 1958, 25-year-old Ronald Marwood, a scaffolder and ex-grammar school boy who'd served two years in the Royal Army Service Corps, celebrated his first wedding anniversary by downing ten pints of ale and getting into a fight outside Grey's Dancing Academy on Seven Sisters Road, north London. Around 40 young men fought each other with weapons including bottles, knives, hammers, knuckledusters and hacksaws. When PC Ray Summers intervened, Marwood stabbed him in the back with a ten-inch knife. Marwood was hanged on May 8 1959. Sources: *Daily Herald*, May 21, 1959; *Daily Mirror*, May 8, 1959; *Villains' Paradise: A History of Britain's* Underworld by Donald Thomas, Pegasus Books, 2006.

108) Digby visits the Ladbroke Grove office of George Rogers MP and his friends argue with Olive Wilson: *Evening Standard*, May 22 1959. The day before, Digby had gone to the House of Commons to arrange the meeting. According to the *Daily Express*, May 22, 1959: *"He [Digby] admitted: 'I lied to the police at first. Just because they've let me out doesn't*

mean they've cleared me. I want the help of a solicitor." The (erroneous, according to Shoggy when I interviewed him years later) report of Breagan taking his girlfriend to a film matinee is from the same source.

109) 'Keep Britain White' rally, Sunday May 24, 1959, see: *The Times*, May 25 1959, *Daily Telegraph*, May 25 1959.

110) The Duke of Edinburgh visits the Rugby Club in Notting Dale: *Daily Express*, May 23 1959, *Prince May Meet Boys Quizzed in Murder Hunt*; *Daily Mail*, May 26 1959, *Murder Quiz Boys Barred on Prince's Tour*; *News Chronicle*, May 26, 1959.

111) The hunt for the knife in the Grand Union Canal: *Evening Standard*, May 25, 1959; *Paddington Mercury*, May 29, 1959.

Silence is the Code

112) A sense of pessimism creeps into the investigation: *Kensington News*, May 22 1959, *Silent Streets Hide a Killer*.

113) Apart from kids calling her "squealer" and other derogatory comments, Joy Okine wasn't threatened - but she'd spoken to the press, and that was enough for the police to consider her at risk. See: *News Chronicle*, May 23, 1959.

114) *"The gangs round here would take revenge on any white person..."* quoted by Edward Scobie in *Black Britannia: A History of Blacks in Britain*, Johnson Publishing Co Inc, 1972.

115) Anonymous letter finds its way to Harrow Road: *Daily Mirror*, May 23, 1959.

116) Police say that 10 witnesses to the killing haven't come forward: *Daily Mirror*, May 20, 1959.

117) Police appeal for the two youths who approached Lewis and Steele as they aided Kelso: *Kensington News*, May 22, 1959; *News Chronicle*, May 20, 1959.

118) Police suggest that two groups of youths could have been involved in the attack: *Daily Mirror*, May 22, 1959.

119) A knife is sent to Harrow Road: *News Chronicle*, May 30 1959.

120) The belief that fascists hadn't simply inflamed feelings in Notting Hill, but had a hand in the murder itself, was fairly widespread, and is still held by some in the anti-fascist movement. The leading article in the Socialist League's newsletter, June 6 1959, for instance, stated: *"Every serious worker should demand answers to the following questions: Who prompted Scotland Yard to issue the statement, calculated to calm public disquiet, that the murder was not committed for racialist motives but for theft? Where did the fascists get the money from to organise the bloody deed? Who at Scotland Yard is covering up for the fascists?"* HO 344/34.

121) Gordon Lewis claims that a far-right group orchestrated the killing: *Sunday Pictorial*, May 31, 1959, *Murder 'A Publicity Stunt' - Thugs hired by political group, police told.* Lewis signs a statement that his claims to the *Sunday Pictorial* are *"completely false"* and Special Branch investigate further: HO 344/34.

Chapter Three: Backstage Manoeuvres

122) Details of the meeting on June 5 1959 in Lord Perth's room in the Colonial Office: CO 1031/2541.

123) Grantley Adams and Philip Rogers biographies: *Oxford Dictionary of National Biography.* Lord Perth biography: *The Times* obituary, November 27, 2002. Garnet Gordon biography: *Who Was Who*, Oxford University Press, December 2007.

124) Claudia Jones and the Inter-Racial Friendship Co-ordinating Council raise £257 for Kelso's funeral. See Marika Sherwood, *Claudia Jones, A Life in Exile*, Lawrence & Wishart, 1999.

125) A Special Branch officer observes Colin Jordan handing out leaflets asking: 'Who Killed Kelso Cochrane?' Source: HO 344/34.

126) Examples of the publicity Jordan attracted include a BBC

Panorama report on April 13, 1959.

127) Special Branch keep tabs on left-wing groups in Notting Hill and log the comments of activist Muzaffa Alijah: HO 344/34. The same Special Branch report also refers to Kelso's funeral service: *"Circulating with these rumours [of police beating up black men at Harrow Road station] is one that alleges that the Bishop of Kensington conducted the funeral of the late Kelso Cochrane, instead of Rev Canon John Collins, because the vicar of the church concerned is anti-colour. The truth is that the Church of England authorities instructed the Bishop to attend because they did not want the service to be led by Canon Collins, whose extreme left-wing sympathies are well known. Stupid though these rumours may seem, they are being seriously considered by the coloured peoples, who in their ignorance of the facts, are easily misled."*

A meeting on 'murder corner'

128) Description of the Union Movement's meeting on the corner of Southam Street, see: Ruth Glass, *London's Newcomers, The West Indian Migrants,* Harvard University Press, 1961. It was Glass who first coined the term 'gentrification' to describe the process of the affluent middle classes displacing the working classes in once poor neighbourhoods. On May 17, 1960, exactly a year after Kelso Cochrane's stabbing Mosley returned to Southam Street and delivered his doom-laden anti-immigration invective through a loudspeaker on the 'murder corner' once more. By now, Glass observed, few outside of Notting Hill took much notice.

129) Although he attracted sizeable crowds during his North Kensington campaign, they were nothing compared to 1930s heyday: at a rally in Birmingham for instance, Mosley once drew 100,000 people: Stephen Dorril, *Black Shirt: Sir Oswald Mosley and British Fascism,* Penguin Global, 2008.

130) 1959 General Election details, see: Stephen Dorril, *Black*

Shirt: Sir Oswald Mosley and British Fascism, Penguin Global, 2008.

131) *"...Of these, only nine threw up any fresh information"*: confidential source.

132) A girl overhears two men talking about the murder in a Notting Hill club: *News Chronicle*, May 23 1959, *Veiled Girl sets off new hunt in Notting Hill.*

133) Newspaper reports on the Dill Joseph Simon shooting: *The Times*, October 20, 1959, *West Indian Shot in Street, 3am incident in Notting Hill; Kensington News*, October 23, 1959, *Talbot Road Shooting; Daily Mirror*, October 20, 1959, *Ginger Girl is Hunted after 3am Shoot Up.* See also: Special Branch report on the shooting, HO 325/9. The same Special Branch note also records the comments of the Trotskyite Bob Pennington at the Socialist Labour League's meeting on Westbourne Park Road: *"In Notting Hill [he said] one negro had been stabbed and another shot at. The police had not been able to discover the culprits. He [Pennington] doubted if they had tried. He then referred to the question of 'Defence Squads', and said that whilst no steps had been taken to form them, these squads may become necessary if violence went on and police proved ineffective..."* Dill Simon's quotes to the *West Indian Gazette* are cited by Marika Sherwood: *Claudia Jones, A Life in Exile*, Lawrence & Wishart, 1999.

134) Dill Simon claimed he strangled Gwen Davies, who was a prostitute, in an argument over money. His appeal against his life sentence was rejected. See: CRIM 1/4169.

135) The question of repatriating Kelso's body rumbles on: CO 1031/2541.

136) *"A forgotten, neglected grave..." Kensington News*, February 26, 1960.

137) Randolph Beresford's conversation with his wife about starting a memorial fund for Kelso comes from *Windrush: The Irresistible Rise of Multi-Racial Britain*, Mike Phillips and

Trevor Phillips, HarperCollins, reissue 2009

138) Beresford's quotes at the unveiling of the Portland grave stone: *Kensington News*, March 11, 1960. Kelso was born on September 26, 1926, not in 1927 as stated on his grave.

139) *"We know who killed Kelso Cochrane - but we can't prove it." Kensington News*, June 3 1960, *Cochrane Killer Is Still Free, Whitsun recalls Murder Charge.*

A Great Patriot

140) Details of Peter Dawson's activities between the end of 1959 and the middle of 1961 are primarily derived from: *The People*, Sunday September 24, 1961, *The Biggest Bully in Britain is Unmasked* by Ken Gardner. See also: *The Times*, June 8, 1960.

141) Dawson was cleared of the charges relating to breaking in and setting fire to the anti-apartheid movement's Bloomsbury headquarters. See: *The Times*, May 11 1961.

142) Dawson and cohorts attack Ghana's High Commissioner after mistaking him for Patrice Lumumba, *Daily Mirror*, August 11 and 13, 1960.

143) The British government sends *"sincere apologies"* to Ghana's leader Kwame Nkrumah for the incident: *The Times*, July 25, 1960. An apology is made in parliament, see: *Hansard*, July 25, 1960, *High Commissioner for Ghana, Assault*. In August 1960 Dawson and two others were found guilty at Bow Street Magistrates Court of the attack outside The Ritz and sentenced to three months in jail. Dawson later lost an appeal against the sentence, *The Times*, August 11 and 13, 1960 and September 22, 1960.

144) In 1961 Patrice Lumumba was murdered in a plot linked to Congo's former colonial power Belgium.

145) Mosley seeks to distance himself from his devotee, and Dawson offers his services to the Ku Klux Klan: *The People*, Sunday September 24, 1961, *The Biggest Bully in Britain is*

Unmasked by Ken Gardner.

146) Dawson claims to know Kelso Cochrane's killer: *The People*, Sunday September 24, 1961, *The Biggest Bully in Britain is Unmasked* by Ken Gardner.

147) Dawson makes a retraction of sorts: A Bully Replies, *The People*, October 1 1961.

148) Dawson is interviewed by the police. They place no reliance on his claims. Confidential source.

149) The Kelso Cochrane case slipped further from public view following Dawson's claims in 1961. Then, on October 19, 1971, the following intriguing little news report appeared in *The Times*: "*Scotland Yard detectives are expected to visit a patient at Broadmoor this week to investigate a new lead in a murder committed 12 years ago. The patient, whose name has not been revealed, has been at the hospital for five years where he is serving a sentence for murder. During a recent conversation with a member of the hospital staff, fresh evidence came to light which may help to solve the murder of Mr Kelso Cochrane, a West Indian who was stabbed during an attack by white youths in north Kensington in May 1959.*" The article wasn't by-lined and the police told me they have no record of anyone at Broadmoor ever being interviewed about the murder.

Chapter Four: More News from Nowhere

150) The Lucretius reference was made in the Appeal Court judgement, Regina v Ram, 1995. It was directed at those campaigners (and perhaps journalists) who struck definitive positions on Ram's innocence from the sidelines, based, in the judges' view at least, on partial and selective evidence. The original Lucretius quote reads: "*Sweet it is, when on the high seas the winds are lashing the waters, to gaze from the land on another's struggles.*"

151) While senior officers in the Lawrence murder inquiry did acknowledge a racist motive in the attack, the Macpherson

report noted that: *"The failure of the first investigating team to recognise and accept racism and race relations as a central feature of their investigation of the murder of Stephen Lawrence played a part in the deficiencies in policing which we identify in this Report. For example, a substantial number of officers of junior rank would not accept that the murder of Stephen Lawrence was simply and solely 'racially motivated'."*

152) The British National Party had offices two miles from where Stephen Lawrence was murdered.

153) The Race Relations Act 1965 forbid discrimination *"on the grounds of colour, race, or ethnic or national origins"* in public places. Areas such as housing and employment were exempt. For this reason, many saw the Act as seriously flawed.

154) Prior to the establishment of the Crown Prosecution Service in 1986 it was incumbent upon the police to assess the evidence and decide whether to prosecute, taking specialist legal advice if they wished. In cases of grave public interest - particularly, as with Kelso Cochrane, homicide before the abolition of the death penalty - the Director of Public Prosecution's office was consulted, and memos outlining the progress of the investigation would be passed up and down a chain reaching up to the Metropolitan Police Commissioner and the Home Secretary. In Kelso's case, this correspondence, which will be contained within the murder case files, remains closed to the public until 2044. No doubt the files will make remarkable reading for some future historian.

155) There's nothing extraordinary in the Cochrane files remaining sealed for so long. Although it's not unprecedented for the files of unsolved cases from this period to be released by the National Archives and the Metropolitan Police, it is rare. The standard objections against disclosure include: that their release might jeopardise "the adminis-

tration of justice", i.e. hamper any possibility of future prosecution; that they contain unsubstantiated and possibly defamatory comments about individuals; the need to protect witnesses; and the distress that their release might cause surviving relatives.

In a test case in April 2007, the Information Commissioner ruled against releasing files relating to the unsolved murder of Jean Townsend, a 21-year-old woman whose body was found on wasteland in Ruislip, Middlesex on September 15, 1954.

156) An insight into police thinking on releasing old murder case files was outlined in *The Times* in March 2010. The paper reported that the Lord Chancellor's Advisory Council on National Records and Archives had decided to remove from public view the case files on the June 1946 murder of a 12-year-old Welsh schoolgirl, Muriel Drinkwater. A police source was quoted: *"As DNA technology advances, more and more of these cases become potentially solvable...We have a real problem with amateur sleuths in this area. There are far too many retired people out there who want to write books about unsolved murders, trawling through these records and coming up with half-baked theories."* The Times, March 30, 2010, *Muriel Drinkwater murder file is declared secret at request of police.*

157) Perhaps the most prominent example of a Ku Klux Klan member convicted decades after his crimes is Edgar Ray Killen. In June 2005, 80-year-old Killen was sentenced to three consecutive 20-year jail terms for his part in the murders of three civil rights activists in Mississippi in 1964.

158) The saga of the *Sunday Express* tip-off, including all the dialogue, comes from MEPO 2/9883.

159) £10 in 1959 equates to around £160 today.

160) The three inquiries into newspaper leaks from within the Met Police's X Division, concerned the cases of Tommy Smithson, Benedict Obibine and a fire at the Mitre Wharf by

the Grand Union Canal. Briefly, for the record:

161) Smithson was a 36-year-old former boxer from the East End who ran prostitution, fencing and protection rackets - "a villain's villain" according to Reg Kray. On June 25 1956, Smithson was shot dead at a brothel in Maida Vale. The press arrived at the scene almost as swiftly as the police. Maltese 'labourer' Philip Elull was sentenced to hang for the crime, but later reprieved. For further detail, see: *Villains' Paradise: A History of Britain's Underworld* by Donald Thomas, Pegasus Books, 2006.

Benedict Obibine, a deeply disturbed Nigerian, barricaded himself into his lodgings at 23 Shrewsbury Road, W2, on March 13, 1957. It took six hours and thirty officers to overpower and arrest him. During the struggle he stabbed PC Charlie Stocker, whose injuries required 32 stitches. As police reinforcements poured into Shrewbury Road, so did the press. The next day's papers carried photos of the saucer-eyed Obibine in a white vest being led off by police, alongside tales of the "Siege of Notting Hill", and eyewitness accounts of the deranged man "pounding up and down in wild war dances and talking in his own tongue". Obibine was later tried for attempted murder. In court he was incapable of following proceedings and claimed that a Ju-Ju priest in Nigeria had told him that a spirit had chosen him for its earthly home, and that if he ever left the country he'd be in mortal danger. The judge sent him down for 14 years.

Finally, in June 1958, the media were again immediately at the scene of the crime, when a fire was started at the Mitre Wharf, a storage site full of old machinery and rubber tyres, by the Grand Union Canal. In each internal inquiry the police source behind the press tip-offs wasn't traced.

162) One old west London lag claims that Johnny Carter avoided the occupational hazard of having the police plant incrimi-

nating evidence on him by getting his tailor to sew up his pockets.

163) For the award of the George Medal to Sidney Coomber, see *The Times*, January 28 1941. As the building around him fell and a slab of stonework hung precariously overhead, Coomber - at great personal risk - tunnelled through the debris to free one of the trapped men.

164) References to Forbes-Leith's investigations into the deaths of Jean Johnson and Fred Skinner: *The Times*, November 7 1959 and December 28 1960.

165) Forbes-Leith leaves the Met: *Daily Telegraph*, February, 27, 1961, *Police Chief to Resign*.

166) Details of Fergie Walker handing the Kray investigation to Detective Superintendent Leonard 'Nipper' Read (who finally brought the twins down): John Du Rose, *Murder Was My Business*, Mayflower Books, 1973. Personal descriptions of Walker: interview with anonymous former colleague of his, August 2009.

167) John Ponder postscript, see *The Times*, February 12 1975, *The Guardian*, May 20 1976, Nick Davies, *Flat Earth News*, Chatto & Windus, 2008.

Chapter Five: Past meets Present

168) Interview at Shoggy Breagan's home and phone conversations: December 2005 - January 2011.

169) Details of Breagan's employment, probation and criminal record: J 200/1

170) Breagan's arrest at a Rachman property: interview with a retired Notting Hill police constable.

171) *Sapphire* was released in 1959, starred Yvonne Mitchell and Nigel Patrick, and was directed by Basil Dearden. It tells the tale of the racist murder of a mixed-race girl, and is said to be partially based on the unsolved killing of Gladys Hanrahan, a 35-year-old (white) woman who lived in St

Ervans Road, W10, and who was found strangled and gagged in Regent's Park on October 1, 1947. A depressingly run-down Southam Street is the setting for a number of scenes.

172) For the GBH on three black men and Judge Aarvold's comments, see: *Kensington Post*, May 17, 1957, *'Vicious Attack' on Coloured Men*.

Wild West Eleven

173) Interviews with Peter Bell, December 2005 - September 2006.

174) The article on Bell and his friends searching Notting Hill for Kelso's killer was in the *Daily Express*, May 20, 1959.

175) Reports on the vast open rubbish dump on the corner of Talbot Grove and St Mark's Road, see: *Kensington News*, August 22, 1958 and September 13, 1957. Talbot Grove was bulldozed out of existence in the wave of slum clearances that swept away much of the old Notting Dale in the 1960s. In its place stands the Lancaster West Estate and Thomas Jones Primary School.

176) Details of Billy Smith's history, his death and the events preceding it: MEPO 2/10063 and DPP 2/3099.

177) Norma Smith interview: *Daily Express*, May 12, 1960.

178) An old Notting Dale resident tells a story that underlines Billy Smith's growing hard-man status in the district. Doogie McGuinness (aka Johnson) was a talented Glaswegian professional lightweight boxer, whose fearsome reputation in the area had been enhanced one night at the Kensington Park Hotel pub (aka the KPH, or 'Keep Paddy Happy'). After belting out a song whose lyrics ran along the lines of "Fuck the Pope", some Irish Catholics present took objection and attacked him. Legend has it that he knocked five of them out. When McGuinness upset Billy Smith and his mates however, things took a different turn. Billy and three friends drove up to Doogie's place in St Stephen's

Gardens, poked their guns out of the window and told him to leave the area. He didn't need further persuasion and left for Glasgow soon after.

179) Descriptions of the Latimer Arms and of the band playing come from one of its old regulars. For its history as a country inn, see: *Notting Hill in bygone days*, Florence Gladstone and Ashley Barker, Anne Bingley Publisher, 1923 and 1969. The Latimer Arm's edifice remains, but the pub closed long ago and the landscape around it has drastically changed, with nearby streets decimated during the building of the Westway dual carriageway between 1964 and 1970.

180) The Three Mrs Bells weep with joy: *Daily Express*, June 30, 1960.

181) Peter Bell died at home on April 14 2009.

Chapter Six: An Unexpected Caller

182) Conversations with Susie Read, July 2006 - January 2010.

183) The documentary *Who Killed My Brother, Kelso Cochrane?* was broadcast on BBC Two in April 2006.

184) John Christie served as a zealous special constable at Harrow Road station during the war, earning two commendations and the sobriquet 'the Himmler of Rillington Place'. No criminal checks were done on his past. If there had been, it would have been discovered that he'd served six months hard labour for beating a woman he lived with and her son with a cricket bat in 1929. Christie ably performed the role of chief prosecution witness at Timothy Evans' trial, and was hanged in 1953. Ludovic Kennedy's 1961 book, *Ten Rillington Place*, was later made into a film starring John Hurt, Richard Attenborough and Judy Geeson, and was a ground-breaking account of a case which was instrumental in the abolition of capital punishment.

Some day

185) Among the speakers at Kelso's graveside was the Notting Hill hustler Michael de Freitas, who later re-styled himself into the revolutionary Michael X, aka Michael Abdul Malik, Britain's supposed answer to Malcolm X. De Freitas finished up more like Charles Manson, his life spiralling into megalomania and murder in his native Trinidad, where he went to the gallows in 1975. The reference to him speaking at Kelso's funeral can be found in the *Souvenir Programme for the Official Lynching of Michael Abdul Malik - with poems, sayings and stories by the condemned*, Compendium, 1973, by Michael Abdul Malik, William Levy and John Michell. See also: John L. Williams' biography, *Michael X - A Life in Black & White*, Century, 2008.

186) Olivia Ellington married in 1960. When contacted, she was understandably reluctant to revisit the traumatic events around Kelso's murder, or her relationship with him.

187) For an hour afterwards hundreds remained by the grave, singing hymns with *"deeply emotional emphasis"*: *The Times*, June 8 1958, *Big Crowd at West Indian's Funeral*.

188) Alfonso Santana created the mosaic. He is also one of the artists behind the mosaic of the Spanish Civil War on Portobello Road.

189) *"...Bob Marley asked us how long shall they kill our prophets?"* David Neita is a barrister and poet.

190) The police never seriously considered Colin Jordan or his White Defence League cohorts as suspects in Kelso Cochrane's murder, and no evidence links them to the crime.

191) Arthur Cook's visit to The Earl of Warwick the day after the murder: *Daily Mail*, May 18 1959, *At Race Murder Corner*.

192) For further detail on Southam Street's demolition after being declared *"unfit for human habitation"*, see: *The Street Photographs of Roger Mayne*, Zelda Cheatle Press, 1993.

193) Prior to the Rev Dr Bertram Peake using the Church on

Golborne Road to house destitute ex-prisoners it served another useful social function as a hostel for local rough sleepers. In 2002 Stella McCartney bought and converted the property for around £2 million.

194) Trellick Tower's story is told in Nigel Warburton's *Erno Goldfinger - the life of an architect*, Routledge, 2004. The Hungarian-born Goldfinger designed Trellick, and had his name appropriated by James Bond creator Ian Fleming, who used it for one of his most famous villains. Goldfinger had a utopian belief in the benefits of high-rise living, and blamed Kensington and Chelsea Council for Trellick's lack of security. For years, the place symbolised the idiocies of high-rise urban planning. Among the most notorious incidents there occurred soon after residents moved in. Just before Christmas 1972 a fire hydrant was let off by vandals on the twelfth floor. Thousands of gallons of water flooded the lift shafts and the entire block went without water, heat and electrical power through the Christmas holiday. In 1984, Trellick Tower was rated as one of the ugliest buildings in the world by the *Financial Times*.

Chapter Seven: Let it Lie

195) 'Frank' is a pseudonym and certain identifying details have been changed.

196) On October 5, 1963, Jordan married Françoise Dior, the French perfume empire heiress. According to Martin Walker in *The National Front*, published by Fontana in 1977, Dior wore a swastika necklace encrusted with diamonds, and the couple toasted the British Nazi Movement to the strains of Horst Wessel Lied. See also: *The Times*, October 7, 1963, *Three Arrested after Wedding Protest*.

197) *"...What evidential value might it hold after so long?"* The question of whether the knife might still be able to be used as evidence: conversations with Professor Allan Jamieson at

the Forensic Institute; Abigail Carter, Forensic Resources Ltd, November 2010 and January 2011.

198) Plans for Pat Digby's old house: planning and conversion department, Kensington and Chelsea Town Hall.

199) Average house price on Princedale Road is £1.6 million. Source: www.mouseprice.com

200) Pat Digby and his friends evading cab fares by running into the Prince of Wales pub and dashing out of the back on to Portland Road. Source: an old friend of Digby's.

Chapter Eight: Afterword

201) A witness identifies Breagan and a companion near the scene before the murder: confidential source.

202) Digby changes his account for his movements on the night: confidential source.

203) Breagan alters his explanation for leaving the party: confidential source.

204) In the *Daily Herald,* May 26, 1959, *Innocent – but I am being pilloried says man in race murder probe,* Breagan is quoted on the different explanations he gave the police for leaving the party, and their decision to release him: *"At the police station I told Det Supt Ian Forbes-Leith I knew nothing about the murder, and that I had been to a party all night, and came out to find some girls. The superintendent said to me: 'You're not telling me the truth. I'll question you again tomorrow.' And they sent me down to the cells to sweat it out. The following day, Wednesday, it was just the same. It wasn't until 6pm when someone came down and said Chief Supt Steve Glander [who had been called in from Number 2 District to help assist the investigation] wanted me. He asked me again what happened on the night of the murder. Then I told him the truth - about the real reason I came out of the party. It was to have a fight with another man at the party but we made it up. Mr Glander said: 'What will happen if you're picked out by one of the coloured men?' [i.e. Lewis or Steele] I told him: 'They*

would pick anyone out so long as he was white.' He said: 'Breagan, I'm thinking it over. Whether to let you go or charge you.' They took me back to the cell to wait for Glander's decision. It was only a five minute wait but it seemed much longer. Then Mr Glander came to the cell and said: 'We haven't grounds for holding you. You're going to be released.'"

205) Witnesses were shown photos of suspects, but no full-blown ID parade was held. A former officer from the time tells me that on the evidence the police had, it should have been.

206) The placing of the suspects in next door cells at Harrow Road: *"Patsy was there. Patsy was in the next cell. I shouted out, 'Patsy what did you tell the police?' He said, 'I told them we were going to have a fight.'"* Breagan interviewed: December 2005.

207) Ian Forbes-Leith's official conclusions on Digby and Breagan: confidential source. He also concluded that after *"weeks of enquiry the majority of those who attended [the party on Southam Street] could be excluded as suspects."*

208) A further police explanation for not charging anyone for the murder is revealed in a note of a confidential meeting about the killing and the situation in Notting Hill, held between the police and West Indian officials on September 9, 1959 at the Commissioner for the West Indies office, 6 Bruton Street, W1. Chief Superintendent Steve Glander (see above), was one of the speakers. The note reads: *"...Chief Superintendent Glander then gave a brief outline of the present position regarding the murder enquiries. He stressed the lack of information which had been forthcoming...and mentioned that the reticence stemmed from all sides, both coloured and white. Mr Glander also qualified and confirmed the assumption that the murder was not racial but that the motive was undoubtedly robbery, as is evidenced by the statement of the two coloured men who found Cochrane immediately after his injuries were inflicted and who heard Cochrane say that the man had asked him for*

money. There was a further point that if racial feeling had been at the bottom of it we would have had no help whatsoever from white residents of the locality. Mr Glander went on to say that two suspects whom police were fairly confident were responsible for the murder were put up for identification but the only eye witness - a cab driver - could not identify them." Source: MEPO 2/9854.

209) *"Joy's mother, Mrs Okine said: "Before the fight started I saw one of the youths try to rip away an iron railing as a weapon, but neither myself nor my daughter saw any knife used."*Source: *News Chronicle*, May 18, 1959. She is also quoted describing the same incident in the *Daily Telegraph*, May 18, 1959, *Kensington Murder Gang Sought*.

210) *"...The disposal of Kelso's clothes, which so perturbed Stanley Cochrane..."* The forensic value Kelso's clothes might have held had they been retained: conversations with Professor Allan Jamieson at the Forensic Institute; Abigail Carter, Forensic Resources Ltd, November 2010 and January 2011.

211) On June 2, 1959 the Home Secretary, the Metropolitan Police Commissioner and the Ministers of Health, Housing and Education met at the Home Office to discuss the Cochrane case and the situation in Notting Hill. Source: HO 325/9. See also: Ruth Glass, *London's Newcomers, The West Indian Migrants*, Harvard University Press, 1960. (Further detail: Source Note 20).

212) At the inaugural meeting of the Socialist Labour League (composed of black and white trade unionists) on May 19, 1959, a resolution was passed to organise defence patrols "to sweep the fascists off the street". *Evening Standard*, May 21, 1959, *Defence body set up*. *"For what they term the 'immediate protection of our persons and property', West African, West Indian and British organizations who are concerned about racial disturbances in Notting Hill and other places have decided to set up defence committee."*

213) Discussions between civil servants and West Indian politi-

cians about repatriating Kelso's body so that his grave wouldn't become a political shrine, but only *"after a reasonable interval"* to *"avoid undue publicity"*, can be found in CO 1031/2541.

214) On August 11, 1959, Garnet Gordon, head of the Commission in the UK for the West Indies, wrote to Philip Rogers, Under-Secretary of State in the Colonial Office. The letter was entitled *Murder of Kelso Cochrane*. It read: *"Kelso Cochrane was murdered on or about 17ᵗʰ of May and this unfortunate event has been much taken to heart by West Indians in the United Kingdom. A great deal of disappointment therefore arises from the fact that up to date no arrests or charges have been made in connection with the crime. Although I have no reason to believe that the Police have been other than diligent in this matter, it would be desirable to have any comment that the Commissioner of Police might be able to make at the present time."*

Two days later Rogers responded in a letter marked PERSONAL: *"...I think you know that all of us here fully understand the feelings of the West Indians about the murder, and share their disappointment that so far no arrest has been possible. You and I both know, however, from the circumstances of the crime how extraordinarily difficult it must be to trace the people concerned and prefer charges against them, and neither of us I am sure has any doubt that the police are doing everything they can..."* The senior civil servant then counselled Gordon against seeking a public response: *"Frankly I am a little worried about the idea of making an official representation through the Home Office in the way your letter suggests, when I am sure that all they can say officially is that they are doing their utmost."* Source: CO 1031/2541.

215) The internal note of Sir Joseph Simpson's conversation with Garnet Gordon on August 27, 1959, is contained in MEPO 2/9854. The relevant section reads: *"...A number of West Indians are asking him [Gordon] what the police are doing about*

it [the murder] and when something is going to happen...I [Simpson] assured him, and he is well aware of the fact, that we were treating this case with the same seriousness that we treat any case, but I hinted to him that, as far as I knew, we had got as far as we could and were balked from taking any further action due to lack of evidence that was unlikely ever to be made good."

216) Yet another demonstration of the official desire to push the case out of the headlines, is revealed in Home Office papers prepared for the Home Secretary for a meeting about racial tension and the situation in Notting Hill, with an all-party deputation of MPs. On June 9, 1959, the group, led by Nigel Fischer, Tory MP for Surbiton, appealed to Butler to *"make a broadcast, on sound and television, appealing to people every-where to appreciate the problems of the coloured immigrants and to avoid actions which may lead to outbreaks of racial violence..."* Source: *The Times*, June 10, 1959. Prior to the meeting a civil servant had suggested to Butler the stance he should adopt: *"The Secretary of State will no doubt take any convenient oppor-tunity of encouraging the doctrine of racial tolerance; but it would surely be a great mistake to stir up fresh interest in the problem of the coloured population by seeking a special opportunity to deal with it."* Source: MEPO 2/9719.

217) Ronald Marwood details: see Source Note 107.

218) The front-page article on Kelso's past: *The People*, May 24, 1959, *Gang Victim Led Double Life*. Comments on Kelso's troubled history appear in various formerly confidential Whitehall letters and memos. For instance, a letter from the Colonial Office to the Administrator's Office in Antigua in July 1959, notes that: *"...More than one of the West Indian ministers over here said that they knew that Cochrane was not one of the more admirable West Indian citizens"*; while a paper by the Committee on Colonial Immigrants refers to Kelso as *"not a wholly admirable martyr"*. See: CO 1031/2541 and CAB 134/1467.

219) Kelso's employer calls him *"an exceptional worker"*: confidential source.

220) I found one overtly racist reference to Kelso Cochrane by the police in the publicly available documents. In his statement to the officers probing the *Sunday Express* newspaper leak, DC Frank Buchan describes hearing a fellow officer on the phone during the early stages of the murder investigation: *"I saw DC Elsdon at the telephone table, phoning somebody I believe it was either the Station officer or reserve man at Harlesden police station, arranging for Sergeants Brittain and Dalziel to be called out and picked up. I heard him mention at the time, probably to the reserve man at Harlesden, that there had been a stabbing and a nigger had been killed."* MEPO 2/9883.

National Archives files:

CAB 134/1467; CO 1031/2541; CRIM 1/3030; CRIM 1/4169; DO 35/7990; DPP 2/3099; HO 344/34; HO 325/9; J 200/1; MEPO 2/10063; MEPO 2/9883; MEPO 2/9854; MEPO 2/9719.

Newspapers, magazines, pamphlets and periodicals:

Acton Gazette and Post; Black and White News; Daily Express; Daily Herald; Daily Mail; Daily Sketch; Daily Telegraph; The Daily Worker; Encounter; Evening News; Evening Standard; Manchester Guardian; Kensington Post; Kensington News; News Chronicle; News of the World; North Kensington Leader; New York Times; Notting Dale - Urban Studies by Tom Vague; The Observer; Paddington Mercury; The People; Shepherd's Bush Gazette; The Star; Sunday Express; Sunday Pictorial.

Select bibliography

Antigua Black, Gregson and Margo Davis, Scrimshaw Press, San Francisco 1973.

A Troubled Area, Notes on Notting Hill, Pearl Jephcott, Faber, 1964.

Beyond the Mother Country, Ed Pilkington, IB Tauris and Co, Ltd, 1988.

Black Britannia: A History of Blacks in Britain, Edward Scobie, Johnson Publishing Co Inc, 1972.

Black Shirt: Sir Oswald Mosley and British Fascism, Stephen Dorril, Penguin Global, 2008.

Claudia Jones, A Life in Exile, Marika Sherwood, Lawrence & Wishart, 1999.

Gangster's Lady, Ellen Cannon, Yellow Brick Publishers, 1993.

Inside Outsider. The Life and Times of Colin MacInnes, Tony Gould, Allison & Busby, 1983.

Jack of Jumps, David Seabrook, Granta Books, 2006.

Jungle West 11, Majbritt Morrison, Tandem Books, 1964.

London's Newcomers, The West Indian Migrants, Ruth Glass, Harvard University Press, 1960.

Memoir of a Fascist Childhood, A Boy in Mosley's Britain, Trevor Grundy, Heinemann, 1998.

Notting Dale 1900 onwards, Nobby Buckingham, Joan Groom, Clara and Jim Garritty - Notting Dale Urban Studies, Kensington Central Library, Local Studies section.

Notting Hill and Holland Park Past, Barbara Denny, Historical Publications, 1993.

Notting Hill in bygone days, Florence Gladstone and Ashley Barker, Anne Bingley Publisher, 1923 and 1969.

Notting Hill in the Sixties, Charlie Phillips and Mike Phillips, Lawrence & Wishart, 1991.

Rachman - the slum landlord whose name became a byword for evil,

Shirley Green, Hamlyn, 1979.

Survey of London, Volume XXXVIII, North Kensington, The Athlone Press, University of London, 1973.

Ten Rillington Place, Ludovic Kennedy, Gollancz, 1961.

The Case of Stephen Lawrence, Brian Cathcart, Penguin Books, 1999.

The Official Encyclopaedia of Scotland Yard, Martin Fido and Keith Skinner, Virgin Books, 2000.

The Stephen Lawrence Inquiry, Report of an Inquiry by Sir William Macpherson of Cluny, February 1999.

The Story of Notting Dale, Sharon Whetlor.

The Street Photographs of Roger Mayne, Zelda Cheatle Press, 1993.

Unhappy Dialogue: The Metropolitan Police and black Londoners in post-war Britain, James Whitfield, Willan Publishing, 2007.

Untouchables - Dirty Cops, Bent Justice and Racism in Scotland Yard, Michael Gillard and Laurie Flynn, Cutting Edge, 2004.

Villains' Paradise: A History of Britain's Underworld, Donald Thomas, Pegasus Books, 2006.

Windrush: The Irresistible Rise of Multi-Racial Britain, Mike Phillips and Trevor Phillips, HarperCollins, reissue 2009.

Acknowledgements

In the winter of 2004, I first learned of the unsolved murder of Kelso Cochrane through a few lines in a book on the history of immigration to the UK. Here was a defining moment in British race relations within living memory, that was now consigned to the footnotes. I was consumed by the idea that the perpetrators were still out there somewhere, and suggested making a documentary on the case to the BBC, where I was then working. Unbeknown to me, Stanley Cochrane had already begun his quest to discover the truth about his brother's death. When the documentary was eventually commissioned, we found Stanley, and he immediately agreed to be part of the programme, which aired in April 2006.

Yet, in some ways, this was unsatisfactory and I felt it couldn't be the final word on the case: there was much more to discover, much more to say. Between jobs, I continued searching for those who might know the answers. As their days ebbed away, many were finally willing to speak, though in some instances only off-the-record; and until fairly late in my investigation, the possibility - albeit distant - of justice finally being done, was real.

But bursting into people's lives and raking over their pasts held dilemmas. The old men I met weren't the violent, testosterone and alcohol-fuelled racist youths of around half a century before. There was the impact of exposure on their families to consider, and just how far should I go in putting long-forgotten criminal records back in the public eye? In the end, such concerns were always superseded by the stark truth that a man's life was taken for no other reason than he was black, and no-one paid for it. To spend months digging into the case, knocking on doors, trying to prise information out of people, then to not put it on the record, would therefore have been an exercise in voyeurism rather than journalism.

In the case of Pat Digby, any libel constraints were lifted by his death in 2007. It didn't relieve me of a duty of fairness: to his reputation, as well as to those still alive who were close to him. In the end, the weight of testimony - not simply from Susie Read or 'Frank', but, compellingly, from someone who was actually present in Southam Street that night - justifies what's written.

In my journey to unravel the past, many have received me warmly. Particular thanks to Stanley Cochrane, who has never sought revenge, only some kind of justice, and Susie Read, who has overcome a great deal in her life and, unlike so many, has been prepared to face the consequences of going on the record about the murder.

I am also, in particular, hugely indebted to Michael Gillard for his unfailing support and wise counsel. Special thanks also to Adrian Gatton, for perceptive advice and giving me the impetus to see this through. For their time, reminisces, knowledge or camaraderie, I am grateful to: Monty Strikes - inimitable still and moving images and generosity with ink cartridges; Gibby Zobel; Maya Cochrane; Rose, Millicent and Chris Christian; Frank and Pauline Pulley, who have shown me much kindness; Derek Jones; the meticulous Zecki Gerloff; Mike Power; Eddie Adams; the late Johnny Edgecombe; the late Roy Stewart; the late Sam Fayne; Jeffrey Smele; Colin Prescod; Dave Pitt; Joe McKenzie; Barry Howe; John Prince; Abigail Carter at Forensic Resources Limited; Professor Allan Jamieson at the Forensic Institute; Alfonso Santana, who is currently at work on an important Southam Street project of his own; Bob Fenton and the Association of Ex-CID Officers of the Metropolitan Police; Geoffrey Braithwaite; the Ken Sprague Fund; Charlie Phillips; Parachute; Pamela Moffatt; Gerry Gable; Madeleine Watson and family; Harry and Kay Fowler; Susan and Rupert Ray; Esther Obiri-Darko; Isabela Yeukai Dampier Spicer; Michelle de Mello and Tom Spicer; Gerry and Tor Adams; the late Helen Maleed; Nisha Ali; Will Davies and family; Steve Barclay; David Malin;

Joan Le Mesurier; Susie Griffiths; Emma Griffiths-Malin; Hemi Sweeney; Fiona Broadfoot; Yolanda Nathan; Tariq Goddard; the Adeyemis; Frank Horwill; Phili Nyoni; Patson Muzuwa; Stephane Gentili; Claudia Stark; Jane Fellner; Anita Bromley; Lee Maddox; Ben Owen; Sean and Kelvin; Geoff Smiles; Martin Herring and Roast Beef TV; the Inn on the Green; Rowan Lawton; Pat Mason; Arlen Harris; Farai Sevenzo and Matthew Collin. Thanks also to the BBC's Fatima Salaria, producer / director of *Who Killed My Brother, Kelso Cochrane?* I am also grateful to many who prefer to remain anonymous, but who generously shared their time and memories.

I have benefitted enormously from the invaluable resources at the National Archives in Kew, the British Library in King's Cross, Kensington Central Library's Local Studies section, North Kensington Library, the British Newspaper Library in Colindale, Westminster Library, the London Metropolitan Archives, Paddington Library, Shepherd's Bush Library, the National Meteorological Library and Kensington Town Hall's Planning Department.

"The past recedes, lapping back from a muddied shore..." Will Self's quote at the start of Chapter Five is from *Walking to Hollywood* (2010), and is reproduced with the kind permission of Bloomsbury and Grove Atlantic.

Contemporary culture has eliminated both the concept of the public and the figure of the intellectual. Former public spaces – both physical and cultural – are now either derelict or colonized by advertising. A cretinous anti-intellectualism presides, cheerled by expensively educated hacks in the pay of multinational corporations who reassure their bored readers that there is no need to rouse themselves from their interpassive stupor. The informal censorship internalized and propagated by the cultural workers of late capitalism generates a banal conformity that the propaganda chiefs of Stalinism could only ever have dreamt of imposing. Zer0 Books knows that another kind of discourse – intellectual without being academic, popular without being populist – is not only possible: it is already flourishing, in the regions beyond the striplit malls of so-called mass media and the neurotically bureaucratic halls of the academy. Zer0 is committed to the idea of publishing as a making public of the intellectual. It is convinced that in the unthinking, blandly consensual culture in which we live, critical and engaged theoretical reflection is more important than ever before.